POLICY AND PRACTICE
NUMBER TWELVE

Drugs

POLICY AND PRACTICE IN HEALTH AND SOCIAL CARE

See www.dunedinacademicpress.co.uk for details of all our publications

POLICY AND PRACTICE IN HEALTH AND SOCIAL CARE

SERIES EDITORS

JOYCE CAVAYE and ALISON PETCH

Drugs

Richard Hammersley

Department of Psychology, University of Hull

and

Phil Dalgarno

School of Health and Life Sciences,
Glasgow Caledonian University

EDINBURGH ◆ LONDON

Dedication
To the memory of David Shewan

First published in 2012 by
Dunedin Academic Press Ltd

Head Office:
Hudson House, 8 Albany Street,
Edinburgh EH1 3QB

London Office:
The Towers, 54 Vartry Road,
London N15 6PU

ISBN 978–1- 906716–11–0
© 2012 Richard Hammersley and Phil Dalgarno

British Library Cataloguing in Publication Data
A catalogue record for this book is available from the British Library

Typeset by Makar Publishing Production
Printed by CPI Group (UK) Ltd., Croydon, CR0 4YY

CONTENTS

The use and misuse of drugs is a classic issue on which many individuals and, even more so, the media will pontificate at length. Yet, despite the authority with which people will pronounce their views, little of the debate is based on knowledge of the variety of activity under the umbrella of drug use or a clear understanding of the evidence base. This volume by Richard Hammersley and Phil Dalgarno, offering a carefully argued and nuanced understanding, is therefore of particular value.

The successive chapters are rooted in the flavour of Scottish culture, searching for an explanation of the particular characteristics of drug use and its management in Scotland. Particular features of this culture are highlighted in the Introduction, before an exploration in Chapter 1 of how the use of drugs came to be constructed as a problem in recent decades. The increasing profile of heroin and the response of the different agencies including criminal justice, primary care and social services are explored. Chapter 2 looks in detail at how drug treatment practices developed in response to the increasing numbers injecting drugs: the development of needle exchanges, the use of substitute prescribing and the provision of specialised treatment services.

The evolution of a Scottish drugs policy is discussed in Chapter 3, an attempt to juggle the demands of criminal justice and health and currently translated in policy terms into the Recovery agenda. Chapter 4 adopts a more reflective stance, suggesting that over time the response to drugs identified as harmful – including tobacco and alcohol – shifts from one of repression to one of accommodation. Finally, in Chapter 5, the authors present their own perspective on developing a rational response to drugs. The moral climate of drug use is complex and the evidence base is often contested. This volume provides an opportunity to understand some of the inconsistencies and intricacies tht lie behind the often incoherent public posturing and debate.

Dr Joyce Cavaye
Faculty of Health and Social Care, The Open University in Scotland, Edinburgh

Professor Alison Petch
The Institute for Research and Innovation in Social Services (IRISS), Glasgow

ACKNOWLEDGEMENTS

We would like to thank our wives Marie Reid and Lindsay Johnson for their support through this project, both as academic colleagues and as domestic allies.

INTRODUCTION

> He ate until he was full, drank seven
> pitchers of the beer, his heart grew light,
> his face glowed and he sang out with joy.
> He had his hair cut, he washed, he rubbed
> sweet oil into his skin, and became
> fully human.
>
> (*Gilgamesh*, trans. Mitchell, 2005, p. 86)

If, in the oldest known work of literature, beer is integral to making a savage 'fully human', how much more engrained could intoxication be into human civilisation? Civilisations have repeatedly received new intoxicants with trepidation and disgust followed by avid enthusiasm, while lawmakers, healers and moralists have worried about their harmful effects and tried to control or ban them (Barr, 1995; Standage, 2007).

This book is not about drugs in their entirety. For good or bad, Scottish policy and practice regarding drugs have mostly been about the problematic use of hard drugs, often by injection, and this is the book's main focus. The book describes how concerns about drug problems arose, and how services and policies have evolved to address problems over three decades, from 1980 to 2010. As well as citing relevant publications we have drawn on our experience and knowledge of the drug scene in Scotland, which dates back to the 1980s.

The book suggests that through necessity Scotland has become relatively good at managing problem drug users effectively and reasonably compassionately, but that it has been less good at managing drugs in the bigger picture. As we will see, drugs 'prevention' remains largely incoherent: there is too little said or done about drug problems that do not concern hard drugs or injecting; scientifically obvious connections between alcohol, tobacco and illegal drugs have be acknowledged only reluctantly; and hesitancy remains about accepting the message of Gilgamesh. Whether we like it or not, intoxication is integral to humankind.

Why Scottish drugs policy is so much about drug injecting

Nowadays, the basics of drugs policy are more often taken for granted or misrepresented than spelled out. Bean (2004) offers an excellent summary of relevant international conventions and treaties. Up until the start of the twentieth century, while there were intermittent concerns about opiates, cannabis and cocaine, there was little systematic effort to control or ban any of these drugs. Controls on the supply of medicines were introduced to prevent the supply of quack medicines (Boussel *et al.*, 1983), rather than to deter people from buying opiates, cocaine or cannabis, which were seen as very useful drugs for pain relief and other purposes.

However, concerns grew about the intemperate and addicted use of opiates, particularly after the invention of morphine (1807), the modern syringe (1853) and heroin (1874). The first international convention on drugs was initially intended to address opiates and cocaine, but the Egyptian representative forced cannabis on to the treaty, making unsubstantiated allegations about insanity and so on that had been soundly rejected by the Indian Hemp Commission (see Schaffer Library of Drug Policy, 2009). Unfortunately, the UK representative was absent from the meeting at the critical moment and could not raise this, so cannabis was included with the other drugs as a political compromise. There cannabis has stayed ever since, despite repeated calls by expert committees for it to be treated differently (Runciman, 1999; RSA, 2007).

What about cannabis?

Cannabis use is much more prevalent than that of any other illegal drug – 10–15 times the number of people admit having taken cannabis as admit to use of any other specific drug (e.g. MacLeod and Page, 2011). Consequently, the majority of people sentenced for drug offences (possession or supply – consumption is not an offence) are sentenced for cannabis, even though cannabis offences are generally prosecuted less determinedly and harshly than for other drugs (see Runciman, 1999; RSA, 2007).

As will be discussed below, in Scotland drug problems are most common among relatively socially excluded people in cities (NHS ISD, 2011). Drug use is more common among other social groups

– middle income groups who are neither the poorest nor the most affluent (SGSR, 2012).

In prevalence and harms cannabis is more like alcohol than like most of the other illegal drugs. For both drugs, use is extensive, common and widely tolerated by other people, even people who do not themselves use it. Like alcohol, serious immediate harms are restricted to accidents and misadventures while intoxicated, including becoming upset and disoriented. One is not comparing like-for-like, but the immediate harms of cannabis appear considerably less than the harms of alcohol (Nutt *et al.*, 2010). The serious long-term physical and mental health harms of cannabis also appear to be considerably less than for alcohol, although there are specific concerns in Scotland about cannabis promoting and sustaining tobacco smoking, because the most common form of cannabis smoking is cannabis resin mixed with tobacco in a large hand-rolled cigarette, a 'spliff' or 'joint' (Amos *et al.*, 2004).

Although the two drugs are similar, referring to alcohol as a drug remains contentious for the alcohol industry and hospitality trade, and policies and practices to control the two are extremely different. Currently, cannabis and other drugs (not forgetting legal highs) that rarely lead to addiction-type problems are in a indeterminate state with concern about them, but a dearth of policies or practices directed at them. We shall propose that this is in part because it is still difficult to have rational public discussions of drugs based on evidence.

The heroin epidemic

The main driver of modern Scottish drug policy was the rapid rise in drug injecting during the 1980s. Compared to the number of unhealthy drinkers or cannabis users in Scotland, there have never been very many injectors, but they tended to be visibly clustered into specific, severely deprived neighbourhoods mostly, to begin with, in Scotland's cities. In Scotland, unlike the rest of the UK, in the 1980s heroin users tended to inject rather than smoke it. They also tended to inject other drugs as well. Visible problems related to drug injecting in the 1980s included an obvious street dealing scene, crime to pay for drugs, discarded drug paraphernalia, HIV infection, overdose and health service use for physical damage done by unhygienic and unsafe injecting practices. Communities, policymakers and journalists found all this horrifying. Injecting grew initially without any systematic infrastructure to plan or run services and interventions against the problem.

Ditton and Taylor (1987) reported that between 1980 and 1984 there was a fairly rapid rise in both new heroin notifications to the UK register of addicts and in heroin-related prosecutions and seizures, which was not mirrored in equivalent rises in other drugs. During this period, most notifications occurred in Glasgow and Edinburgh, but Dundee and Aberdeen notifications began to rise quickly about 1985. Ditton and Taylor (1987) also noted a great diversity of services for drug users, and these are discussed further in subsequent chapters.

Welcome to Scotland

Much of the geography of Scotland, made famous by tourism, is rural and romantic with low population densities. Yet about three and a half million of the total five million population live in, or within relatively rapid travel of, its two large cities: Edinburgh (population 446,110); and Glasgow (population 577,980), which are only forty miles apart. About another one million live in or near Aberdeen or Dundee, leaving only about half a million people scattered across the Highlands, the Borders and other predominantly rural areas. As in most countries, rural Scotland is often more conservative (and less socialist in politics) than urban Scotland. Rural Scotland is the common image of the place, but most inhabitants live in the megalopolis comprising Edinburgh, Glasgow and the places around them. Within the megalopolis, as in others such as London or Sheffield–Leeds–Bradford, people commonly travel some distance to work and to access services and leisure facilities.

Both cities have tourist-attractive amenity-rich city centres. Both also have large more peripheral areas of much less attractive twentieth-century housing, including some highly deprived areas, such as large housing schemes built to alleviate inner-city overcrowding. The surrounding towns and villages include many that grew up in the industrial era, producing cloth, coal, steel, ships, cars and so on, then went into post-industrial decline starting in the 1970s. Now in the early twenty-first century they are beginning to transform and regenerate. It was this urban and post-industrial geography that formed a 'land fit for heroin' in the 1980s.

Drug use and drug problems emerged in the cities, then diffused to the surrounding towns, villages and countryside. Many rural areas of Scotland also experienced post-industrial decline, with the loss or reduction of traditional industries such as cloth manufacturing and fishing. The proportion of people living in poverty in rural Scotland is only slightly lower than in urban Scotland. In both, there are marked differences between areas, and often adjacent neighbourhoods can have markedly different deprivation rates (see Scottish Government, 2012). The common problems of rural poverty and social exclusion include transport difficulties, isolation, insufficient demand to maintain local services, and travel difficulties to services that are further away (see EKOS, 2009). These issues apply to all services from shops to highly specialised services: for example, a problem drug user who lives rurally may be unable to attend a service that offers daily on-site methadone.

Social life outside the home has long placed a heavy emphasis on 'the pub', particularly for men (see, e.g., Wight, 1993). This may mean an actual 'public house', but it may also entail going to a hotel, a sports club such as a golf or bowling club, another type of club with membership, or indeed to an unlicensed shebeen selling alcohol, or simply to a 'drinking house' whose alcoholic occupants welcome pretty much anyone bringing a bottle. While many Scots are keen on outdoor activities, even these often begin, or end, in the pub, for simply 'hanging out' alfresco can be unappealing in rain, darkness or when plagued with midges.

Scotland had a strong temperance tradition. Historically there were dry towns, villages and islands, without public houses. Naturally, as with drugs, the stronger was the temperance, the more behind closed doors was the drinking. Temperance has gradually eroded since the First World War and despite continued traditions of Christian temperance in places, and new traditions of Islamic temperance, nowadays more than 90% of adult Scots drink alcohol.

Health professionals were pointing out the problems caused by drink long before drugs arose as an issue and have continued to do so. It is only since the turn of the twenty-first century that their concerns have been much listened to, because of an alarming rise in alcohol intake and drink-related problems (Leon and McCambridge, 2006). Heavy drinking to intoxication is not unusual (Forsyth *et al.*, 2005).

This book uses 'inebriation' to refer to drug or alcohol use that suffices to cause some psychoactive effects, but not necessarily with overt impairment or effects discernible to others, and 'intoxication' to refer to use that additionally causes overt impairment, dysfunction and loss of control over intake. Distinguishing the two conditions is important whatever the drugs.

Many people who are regularly inebriated reject the idea that they are dependent on alcohol or drugs, because they are not regularly intoxicated. This applies to methadone users (Hammersley and Dalgarno, 2012), long-term heavy cannabis users (Coggans *et al.*, 2004) and untreated heavy drinkers (Webb *et al.*, 2007).

Traditions of inebriation and intoxication can extend to a perverse pride in unhealthy excesses. People boast about excessive drinking and laugh about some of the bad consequences. Mullen (1993) interviewed Glaswegian men and identified links between masculinity and excess which are probably not special to Glasgow. Men 'should' be able to push things to the limit. Moreover, being fit and healthy, for instance by exercising or playing sport strongly, licenses the man to be fit to handle greater excesses. Thus, not being able to drink 'properly' on occasion, eating 'rabbit food' or having to watch one's weight suggest lack of manliness. Moreover, participants expressed the commonly held idea that health was a sort of bank where one could increase health by increasing healthy behaviours, then make a withdrawal by doing something unhealthy. Commonly, deposits are made during the week and withdrawals are made at the weekend.

The theory of heroin use as a career (Agar, 1973; Maruna, 2008) mirrors these ideas – that being able to handle a life of excess and danger can be valued positively. Drug subcultures contain their own comedy and battle stories about the misadventures caused by intoxication. Rather than simple issues of health, being able to keep a heroin habit going seems to involve issues of toughness and competence. People quit the life in part because they feel that they no longer have the capacity for it (Anderson and Levy, 2003). Seeking to get so drunk as to blackout and seeking to get so wasted on heroin that one is 'gouching' and nearly unconscious are both examples of intoxication.

Drugs before the heroin epidemic

If alcohol provided the foundation for drug issues in their modern form, drug use during the 1970s in Scotland provided the keystone. There is little officially written or known about drug use during that decade, but it was there in the cities. As in many places in the 1960s and 1970s, it was largely limited to students, intellectuals, music lovers, arty types and so on. Conventional working-class youth generally frowned on it, at least to begin with, unless they gravitated into the proper circles and became 'freaks', which is what Scottish drug users called themselves then, although the definition and application of 'freak' were hotly contested.

The mainstay of the drug scene was cannabis, as it still is today. People also took amphetamines, barbiturates, benzodiazepines (when they became available), LSD, magic mushrooms and cocaine. Hallucinogens were often considered to be 'good' mind-expanding drugs. Others were viewed with more caution. Being a freak involved being an informed consumer, at least in theory. Opiate use was rare, and heroin was barely available. Cocaine supply was unpredictable and expensive. Freaks usually also drank alcohol. Some saw drugs and alcohol as largely incompatible; most did not except in so far as alcohol tended to deaden some drugs' psychedelic and hallucinatory effects.

The move of youth culture away from hippy to punk in the late 1970s is often portrayed as a dramatic shift, but at least in Scotland it was mainly a shift of fashion. Freaks objected to punks' lack of positive values, but they shared disaffection with mainstream culture and many people switched styles and music without altering their substance use in any significant way. However, punk seemed to appeal more widely to working-class youth who had previously looked down on freaks. Drug use continued to spread outwards from the cities and outwards from a counterculture minority. Moreover, while freaks had sometimes appreciated the spiritual, contemplative, mind-expanding aspects of drugs, punks went more for a reckless hedonism that was even less compatible with sensible use.

The heroin 'epidemic' is sometimes described as hitting previously drug-naïve populations. While it did take root most strongly in deprived communities that had probably used drugs less than more affluent ones, urban Scotland in general already had a range of drug and alcohol experience to build on.

Scotland's 'schemes'

We need to conclude by discussing the physical and social environments in which drug injecting first became common in Scotland. The seedbeds of heroin injecting in the housing schemes of Edinburgh, Glasgow, Dundee and Aberdeen look grim and in the 1980s they looked worse, for there have been efforts made since to renovate them, parachute in private housing schemes, and provide exterior decoration and vegetation. On the other hand, it was, and still is, generally safe to get out of your car in one of these areas.

When you do, you will mostly meet white Scots because there is very little ethnic dimension to poverty in Scotland. This is entirely different from North America or some English cities. With recent immigration, many schemes contain some people from other ethnic backgrounds, but drug use is not particularly an issue with them. Moreover, although Scots can be as racially prejudiced as anyone else, much of their bile is directed at the English or at people from Glasgow (or Edinburgh), and there is a fading but still serious sectarian divide between Protestants and Catholics, perpetuated by the sectarian roots of some of the main football teams. This seems to be worse in the west of Scotland, but this is probably only because there are fewer people of Catholic origin in the east. Prejudice against people of colour, or 'Pakis' (e.g. from Pakistan, although the word used to be applied to anyone with a brown skin), is sometimes expressed, but people from southern Asia do not play a significant role in the drugs problem either.

So, the people who live on Scottish housing schemes and other areas of bad housing are stigmatised only by their postcodes. However, the UK being the class-ridden country it is, people, including law-enforcement officers, try to spot deprived people on the basis of their clothing, accents, names, general comportment and consumer choices.

Many of the schemes where drug injecting got started included concrete low-rise flats and high-rise flats built badly in the 1960s. Poor construction meant problems such as damp were common.

Much of this accommodation was owned by local councils and rented cheaply to working-class tenants, so at one point in the 1970s Glasgow's director of housing described himself as the biggest slum landlord in Europe.

As Scotland lost industry and mining, council tenants became particularly likely to be unemployed. This was not a uniform problem because different areas and 'schemes' had different amenities and social status. Tenants needed more points to get tenancies in more prestigious areas. Consequently, the worst areas, where 'anyone' could get a tenancy, tended to be inhabited predominantly by those with most acute problems and fewest points, including the homeless, those who had previously lost tenancies – sometimes through drink, drugs or misbehaviour – and those who were simply young and had not built up many points in the system. The 'worst' schemes tended to go into a downwards spiral, as many of the more aspirant or respectable residents left. Over the years, at some point many of the really bad schemes were targeted for regeneration. This often worked to some extent, but as the area became more desirable the people with fewest points (including those with the most problems) tended to be displaced to another bad area that spiralled down in turn.

However, many deprived schemes, towns and areas also attracted and continue to attract considerable loyalty from their residents. Researchers often find that residents express understandable distaste, frustration and anger at the local lack of amenities and sometimes squalid living conditions that they face, but that many consider the local people to be wonderful, loyal, community people. A sting in the tail of these positive attitudes used to be that the 'wonderful locals' often excluded immigrants, junkies, alcoholics, single mothers and so on, who actually lived in the community in large numbers.

Excluding them has long been rather an unrealistic view of community, because most extended Scottish families include at least one unwed mother (and usually a single parent as well), one or more people with alcohol problems and, nowadays, somebody with a drug problem. What has changed is that some of these behaviours are not covered up as much as they used to be.

Conclusions

Drug problems developed in Scotland because they were compatible with existing traditions of inebriation and intoxication, although as we will see when heroin appeared it was perceived to be alien. Also, because Scotland has notable problems of relative poverty, deprivation and unemployment, problem drug use could develop easily there.

CHAPTER 1

The Invisible Junkie: Constructing the Modern Drugs Problem

The British model

Before the 1980s the 'British model' of the management of opiate users was frequently held up as a paradigm of good practice (see Strang and Sheridan, 1997 for summary). Opiate addicts could register with a doctor and be prescribed opiates for personal use. However, there were under 700 people registered up until the 1960s; most used morphine rather than heroin; and most were either therapeutic addicts who had used morphine for pain relief, or professional addicts such as doctors or nurses. In the first half of the 1960s a growing number of younger people went on to the register, seeded by a number of Canadians who moved to England to get heroin prescriptions and worsened by liberal prescribing of heroin to them, primarily by one doctor. Partly in response to these excesses, from 1968 only licensed doctors could prescribe heroin and gradually the number of methadone prescriptions increased, while the number of heroin prescriptions stayed constant, low, and was a reducing proportion of the total number of prescriptions. Up until 1996, when the register of notified addicts was replaced by other ways of recording problem drug users, there was also a long gradual increase in the number of people registered.

Registered addicts received prescribed morphine, diamorphine (heroin), another opiate or, sometimes, other drugs. This allowed them to live relatively stable lives, to avoid incessant use of the black market and to avoid persistent, habitual crime to fund black market heroin. It also meant that addicts could receive drugs of good quality and inject or otherwise consume them hygienically and safely. The arguments in favour of the British model were that it reduced crime by opiate addicts by reducing their need to afford and buy black market opiates and that it allowed monitoring and stabilisation of health problems related to opiate injecting. In the 1960s perhaps half the people known to drugs treatment services were on the register, but this proportion probably declined as the years went by and, as heroin become more widely used, there were probably more heroin users not known to treatment services. As needle exchanges were set up it became apparent that clients included large numbers of people who had never been arrested, or sought help for their drug problems (Frischer *et al.*, 1997).

As described in the Introduction, between the 1950s and 1970s more diverse recreational drug use gradually emerged in the UK, and this was not manageable by 'registering addicts'. There was much more cannabis use than other drug use: Plant (1975) called his book on cannabis users *Drug-Takers in an English Town*, because the drug-takers in the location that he studied were predominantly cannabis users. Other than that study and a few surveys, there was very little published research on recreational drug use in the UK. There was more concern about the adverse effects of barbiturate abuse, which had largely disappeared by the 1980s.

There was no perceived need for psychiatric services for recreational drug users, although psychiatrists occasionally saw people suffering from psychotic symptoms induced by cannabis, amphetamine or hallucinogen use. Addiction psychiatrists tended to treat both people with alcohol problems and people dependent on other drugs, and there were many more of the former, just as there are today. General thinking was that substance-use problems were problems of individual mental health, which could be treated by substitute prescribing and individual psychological therapy of some kind, although some registered addicts stayed in treatment for decades. However, heroin use gradually increased.

The heroin epidemic
Things had begun to change by the beginning of the 1980s. Heroin became much more widely available as brown heroin started to be

imported from the Middle East in large quantities. Unemployment in the UK among sixteen to twenty-four year olds stood at nearly 20% (Bell and Blanchflower, 2010). In Scotland, unemployment rates tended to be highest in the housing schemes described in the Introduction. Heroin became available in those schemes, as in many deprived areas of the UK, and people began to use it.

There were fewer specialised addiction psychiatrists than there are today, and most addictions services, which tended to be based in psychiatric hospitals, worked mainly with people with alcohol problems. Similarly, the police in Scotland had been used to dealing with drug offences in general, but until the 1980s drug offences did not often mean heroin. Policy and services were not well organised to think about and cope with a rapid increase in the number of people injecting drugs. This change became visible in a number of ways. First, the police and prisons began to notice that a large proportion of people arrested and imprisoned for theft and other crimes were heroin injectors. This was obvious because they had injecting equipment and/or drugs in their possession, because they admitted to heroin use or said that they had offended to buy drugs, because they showed withdrawal symptoms, or because they had the physical marks of injecting. Second, addiction services started seeing more people seeking help for heroin addiction. Third, nonspecialist parts of the NHS started treating people with a variety of problems related to drug injecting, such as abscesses, other infections and drug overdoses. Roy Robertson (1987), a GP in a deprived area of Edinburgh, was among the first to start formally recording drug injecting among the patients attending his practice. Fourth, in some areas heroin dealing became quite visible on the street both to local residents and to the police. Alongside signs of dealing often came also discarded drug paraphernalia, such as used syringes.

Drugs other than heroin were involved from early on. Particularly in Glasgow, buprenorphine (usually called 'tems', short for the brand name Temgesic) and temazepam were often used. The latter is a benzodiazepine commonly prescribed to aid sleep, often known as jellies on the street because it came in gel-filled capsules. Both drugs had been heavily marketed as safe medicines.

It is likely that both drugs began to be used by enterprising drug injectors who had access to other people's prescriptions, or indeed to their own, because both drugs were sometimes prescribed by GPs to help addicts stop heroin use. Once the word got around that you could get intoxicated on tems and jellies, some people with prescriptions started selling them. There were also over the years a number of major thefts from chemists and of entire lorry loads of the drugs, which being widely prescribed were delivered in large quantities. Cocaine was relatively speaking a rarity, while amphetamine injecting never really took off in Scotland, although it became common as near as Manchester (Klee, 1992).

By 1985 there was sufficient concern about the heroin epidemic that a number of research projects were funded to study it (Hammersley *et al.*, 1989; McKeganey and Barnard, 1992a; Haw, 1985; Taylor, 1994). At that time, the main problem was surmised to be ignorance about the highly addictive nature of heroin, leading to people becoming addicted unwittingly: for example, the slogan of the somewhat naïve 1985 media campaign was 'Heroin screws you up', as if nobody knew.

The heroin problem was described in the media, and by many politicians, as to be so serious as to require a substantial, urgent response. But what response was there, and indeed what was the nature of the problem? It was correctly assumed that the injecting epidemic had created unknown thousands of heroin addicts. Presumably, the nature of heroin addiction was largely unchanged from previous decades and should be tackled in similar ways: by stifling the supply of heroin; and by registering and prescribing to addicts. An immediate and obvious difficulty was that there appeared to be thousands of new opiate users and almost no capacity to deal with them. Moreover, specialist addiction services tended to be in psychiatric hospitals, which new heroin users were reluctant to attend.

Specialist treatment
In the early 1980s, for example, one psychiatric addiction service in Glasgow had five beds for drug addicts on a ward primarily for alcoholics, for a catchment area that included several schemes thought each to contain at least hundreds of new drug injectors. Throughout

Scotland, there was a severe scarcity of treatment places relative to the number of people who might require treatment.

Consequently, other services sprang up. By 1986, these included some services in the community, a few of these were funded in 1983 with grants totalling half a million pounds from the Scottish Office. Some were primarily financed by social work departments, and some residential services were supported by various charities, including religious ones. Other services were set up by one or two dedicated and determined individuals, and became charities afterwards. All were short of funds, adequately trained staff and appropriate accommodation. For example, for a few years a service was operating from an abandoned and semi-derelict seminary some way west of Glasgow. Narcotics Anonymous was barely present in Scotland, although twelve-steps principles were known and used by many services.

Several of the services that began during this period are still going in various forms. The main focus was on recovery (although the word was used somewhat differently then) from addiction – getting people off drugs. This could be achieved in the community, with sufficient support such as was offered by many mutual help organisations, one famous one being Calton Athletic. Or, it could be done more intensively in a residential programme. By and large, the physical health problems of drug injecting were seen as secondary. So the agendas of meeting drug users' health care needs and getting them off drugs tended to run in parallel and often barely communicated with each other. One person, for example, might be getting excellent assistance towards recovery, but struggle to get health care needs met. Another might be well cared for by their GP, but be unable to get a place in rehab.

Primary care
There were essentially no policies or good practice guidelines for the management of drug 'addicts' in primary care. Fairly suddenly, primary care practices whose catchment areas included deprivation were seeing not just one or two but sometimes dozens of people who injected drugs.

A few practices, notably Roy Robertson's practice in Edinburgh, rapidly became exemplary for providing the complex care and support that drug injectors can require, which will be detailed shortly. Some practices apparently adopted discriminatory practices against drug injectors, on the grounds that they were dangerous, difficult, disruptive and dishonest patients (which they sometimes were) that required special facilities to treat. If the injector attending such a service was lucky, they were referred to a local specialist service, whether that was an NHS psychiatric service or a third-sector service of some kind. If the injector was really lucky then the service had a place for them. Most were simply placed on a waiting list. More sensible injectors tried to change their GP. This meant that more sympathetic practices could feel overwhelmed with drug injectors.

Most practices provided some care, probably had more drug injectors registered with them than they knew, and muddled along with no systematic support, no clear guidelines for the management and treatment of addiction and drug injection, and sometimes less knowledge of the problems than was ideal. Only relatively few GPs would prescribe methadone because of concerns about replacing one addiction with another, being unable to provide the psychotherapeutic counselling that should accompany substitute prescribing (Seivewright, 2000) and being inundated with opiate users wanting prescriptions.

Some drug injectors interviewed in the 1980s in Glasgow reported being prescribed benzodiazepines supposedly to help them detoxify, although they were often already consuming large quantities of black market temazepam or diazepam orally or by injection. Some GPs tried prescribing other opiates instead of methadone, including codeine preparations – the logic for this was never clear – and buprenorphine, which was then being marketed as an analgesic with low abuse potential. Indeed, it is now in wide use as a prescribed substitute drug, partly because there is a low probability of overdose (Hammersley *et al.*, 1995). These prescribing tactics collectively underestimated the perverse resourcefulness of drug users, who at the time were commonly abusing buprenorphine, which was easily injected because it came in soluble form, and were taking large multiples of the therapeutic doses of temazepam and diazepam.

Criminal justice

The police and prison service saw that a very large proportion of arrestees and new inmates not only showed overt signs of drug injecting such as needle marks, but also exhibited withdrawal symptoms of varying severity after some time in custody. Police surgeons and prison medical services had neither the staff nor the facilities to handle this as a routine matter. Prisons were frustrated at the large number of drug injectors incarcerated for relatively minor crimes such as persistent theft or shoplifting, because they felt that were these people treated perhaps they need not return to prison yet again. There was considerable discretion, confusion and inconsistency in the management of drug injectors. One example of confusion was that Lothian Police (Edinburgh) tended to confiscate injecting equipment, while Strathclyde Police (Glasgow) often did not (Robertson, 1987), which may have affected the different rates of HIV infection in the two cities.

Throughout the 1980s prisons tended to use very conservative practices regarding the prescribing of psychoactive drugs, whatever the medical reasons, although purportedly Scotland's prison for women – Cornton Vale – was more inclined to prescribe. Consequently, dependent opiate users tended to have to withdraw unassisted in prison, although if the prison knew that they were dependent they would be placed on close watch for the first few days. Opiate users receiving methadone prescriptions often had these cut off on entry to prison, and if they received methadone at all it was on the basic of a rapid reduction of dose for detoxification.

At the same time, the prevalence of drugs in prison was increasing (although accurate data on this was not available until much later, when random drug tests were introduced) and there were growing problems of the sharing of injecting equipment. (These issues will be considered further in Chapter 2.) The prison system felt stuck between the problems of managing prison security and preventing illegal behaviour, and looking after prisoners' mental and physical health. To begin with, the prevention of illegal behaviour generally had priority.

The courts were also confused about how to sentence offenders who had drug problems. In Scotland, minor offences are judged by sheriffs (who are lawyers, unlike English magistrates, who are trained lay people). Anecdotally, some sheriffs were believed to consider drug addiction as a mitigating circumstance, leading to a non-custodial disposal. Others were believed to view drug addiction as an aggravating circumstance and were believed to be more likely to imprison known drug users for relatively minor offences. The situation deteriorated to the point that, when some defendants turned up at court and realised that a tough-on-drugs sheriff was on duty, they fled before their case came up, taking their chances with arrest warrants for non-appearance and hoping that next time they would get a more lenient judge. Tactical appearance still goes on.

For much of the 1980s there were also regional variations in the practices of procurator fiscals (the prosecuting lawyers). In regions where there were perceived to be few problem drug users such as, initially, Tayside and Grampian, possession of heroin or cocaine was regarded as a serious offence and a custodial sentence was sought, with the aim of keeping drugs out of the area. In Glasgow or Edinburgh possession of a modest amount of any drug usually led to a fine.

The 1980s saw a steady rise in Scotland's prison population, mostly reflecting crime by drug users. But, when most criminals use drugs, causality is not straightforward and both occur in a common causal nexus including poverty, educational, social and psychological problems (e.g. trauma), what is now called 'social exclusion' and family dysfunction. Sensible prison officers have long realised that prison is a last disposal for people who often have multiple problems other than the crimes that they received custodial sentences for. Drugs added considerably to the list of common problems in prison.

Social services
Social services were the main funders of many of the community services for drug users. Additionally, social services were and are often involved in the many problems that drug injecting could contribute to, including problems with physical or mental health, imprisonment, child welfare issues and housing problems, as well as the difficulties that precede and go along with a person developing a drug (or alcohol) problem. These include: any of the preceding problems for the parents or other family members; truancy and other

educational issues; parental, or sibling, alcohol or drug problems; breakdown of parental relationships; domestic and child abuse; and children being taken into care. Because of the furtive and stigmatised nature of opiate use, social workers did not always know that they were working with drug injectors. In cases with such complex issues, people may have special reasons to conceal drug use, if they can. Also, in such challenging situations drug use may not be the most pressing priority.

Nowadays, most social workers probably have a fairly clear understanding of drug use as opposed to drug injecting and drug dependence. In the 1980s many did not because the relevant training was only getting started and because the generic reaction to 'drugs' was to refer people to a specialist service. Consequently, clients were very cautious about disclosing drug use to social workers.

As the heroin epidemic developed it was widely believed that being a 'junkie' made it particularly likely that your children would be placed in care. It is not clear that this was ever true in Scotland, compared to say neglecting children due to alcoholism, but it is true that drug injectors, indeed drug users in general, often did their best to conceal or downplay their drug use from fear that they would lose their kids if it were known (Taylor, 1994).

Drug problems and other issues

At that time, being a 'junkie' or having one in the family was seen as particularly shameful and extreme anti-junkie sentiments were widely expressed. A recurrent theme was suggesting that they should all be exiled to an island. Another common theme, which has impeded rational drugs policy ever since, was to regard heroin as uniquely addictive and problematic. Off the record, we have been told of families who blamed the family's entire dysfunctionality on the junkie member, despite the massive multiple problems of other family members, often including serious, enduring alcoholism.

Also, working with such complex cases, it can be unrealistic to seize on one key problem that is the root of all the other difficulties. Typical social work practice – and hence early drug service practice – was, and remains, more influenced by psychodynamic theories than is the everyday practice of NHS services for drug problems.

In psychodynamic terms, a drug or alcohol problem is more of a symptom of deeper psychological issues than it is the cause of a person's problems (e.g. De Paula, 2004). On the other hand, when a person has an enduring dependence on drugs or alcohol, then it is advisable to treat dependence first (Beck *et al.*, 1993; Vaillant, 1995). This is partly because it is treatable compared to other mental health problems, partly because chronic inebriation can interfere with psychological therapies, and partly because common psychological problems such as depression and anxiety can be worsened by drug or alcohol use and alleviated by getting a drug problem under control.

Assessment

It is important that each person's drug use and drug problems are understood and addressed within the broader context of their lives. This requires detailed, competent assessment of individual cases. In early services in Scotland, there could be little or no competent documented assessment. Some workers were coy about assessment because they believed asking questions would damage rapport, or cause clients to disengage. (The nature of competent assessment will be discussed in Chapter 4.)

Early difficulties

The early response to heroin/drug injecting involved fear, alarm and prejudice. There was a widespread hope that it would go away or die down again. The police contributed to this hope by making what now look like wild promises to eradicate drugs, attracting further resources to this end: for example, in about 1987, Strathclyde police received funding for a helicopter – much needed for various aspects of police work – on the argument that they required it to tackle drugs. It was never clear how one uses a helicopter to find heroin, or heroin dealers (cannabis farms being a decade or so in the future), but they got the money anyway.

Drugs prevention and treatment work was underfunded and barely planned at all. The primary provider of drugs education was the police, as it had been since the 1970s. As every schoolboy knows, the police have a specific agenda on drugs that does not necessarily mesh well with the agenda of young people at risk of drug trying.

Moreover, drugs education did not prevent young people using drugs (Coggans *et al.*, 1991). Most services had to renegotiate their funding from year-to-year and faced annual worries that they would be unable to continue to operate.

There were also difficulties with three simplistic ideas about what might work for heroin dependence. One such idea was that because heroin dependence could be attributed to the sheer addictiveness of heroin, all that was required was that addicts were detoxified of heroin, typically over a period of about six weeks, although sometimes more rapidly. Once free of heroin the brain could return to normal and the person would no longer want or need heroin. Unfortunately, opiates affect brain function for longer than this (Everitt *et al.*, 2001), and detox underestimates the pleasurable allure of heroin, its use to cope dysfunctionally with life's problems and systemic factors in heroin use. Detox without much psychological treatment tends to lead to relapse (Simpson and Friend, 1988).

Another simplistic idea was that abstinence was the primary goal of treatment and that abstinence was best achieved with some form of twelve-steps influenced intervention. As a self-help movement, Narcotics Anonymous has considerable strengths, although evidence for its effectiveness is more limited than the evidence for Alcoholics Anonymous (McKellar *et al.*, 2003). But there are key differences between self-help and treatment. Self-help movements encourage members to work towards abstinence but tolerate relapse and offer support. Self-help movements usually occur in the community, or in prison. In the 1980s, most twelve-steps abstinence-oriented treatment in the UK occurred in residential therapeutic communities.

Existing ones were fairly hastily expanding their remit from alcohol to include drugs, others were being established by enthusiasts in recovery, who did not necessarily have advanced business planning or service organisation skills. Indeed, while most had experience of drug use, or of drug users in their family or community, many did not have even basic knowledge or training in addictions. Of course, by combining simplistic idea one with simplistic idea two, abstinence becomes simple; the person stops using drugs and gets better. Facilitating this does not necessitate advanced psychotherapeutic or pharmacological expertise.

Often, residential treatment required that the person stay drug free, and anyone who did not manage this was discharged. This meant that the graduates of such residential treatment consisted entirely of people who were capable of abstaining from drugs for the duration of the programme, making abstinence a kind of self-fulfilling prophecy, if one ignores both the people discharged and the people who did not get a place because they lacked the motivation to become abstinent (Miller and Sanchez-Craig, 1996).

Unfortunately, with abstinence as the primary goal of treatment, services for the people in the community not as yet capable of abstinence were not seen as a priority. Indeed, the normal reaction of generalist health and social care services was to refer anyone who seemed to have a drug problem to the first specialist drug service that they could think of. At least, there was no evidence that referral was any more systematic than this (Ditton and Taylor, 1987).

Service evaluation of any kind was rudimentary in the 1980s, and the remit of community services could be unclear. More than one community service recorded every person who came through the door to be a 'client', whether this was their first or hundredth visit, so services seemed to have a lot of clients. That was sometimes the only data collected, on the dubious rationale that without complete confidentiality clients would not appear at all.

The third simplistic idea about what might work for heroin dependence was that substitute prescribing constituted a treatment for heroin dependence, rather than simply being a form of palliative care. It seemed logical to give methadone in the community until such time as the person 'was ready' to be abstinent. But there was little focus on how to facilitate such readiness – which nowadays would be seen as the mainstay of competent treatment.

The main initial problems were huge gaps in skills and resources. Heroin users were lucky to get any treatment at all, and fortunate if they were cared for relatively compassionately by local NHS services when they required medical care. There had however been a national training programme for voluntary alcohol workers in Scotland since the 1970s, and training programmes had been set up for drug workers also, with the universities of Paisley (now University of West Scotland) and Stirling being important. The impact of training was not immediate, and drug workers in practice might have only rudimentary knowledge of different drugs or of how to use psychological interventions.

Public health and HIV

From 1981 onwards awareness of AIDS was growing. Drug injecting has been a much more common route of infection in Scotland than in the rest of the UK. Up to the end of 2010 in Scotland 22.5% of diagnoses of HIV were due to drug injecting, compared to 4.7% for the UK as a whole (Avert, 2012). Moreover, Scotland had 24.7% of the UK's cases of HIV infection due to drug injecting, despite having under 10% of its population.

The involvement of public health relatively early on in Scotland's heroin epidemic transformed thinking about drugs problems and responses to them. It was helpful that the heart of public health is epidemiology, which involves counting things, rather than relying on clinical intuition to guess what works. In contrast, the heroin epidemics in the USA in the 1960s and 1970s occurred well before AIDS, and the assumption that drug addiction was a problem of individual psychopathology and morality entrenched largely unchallenged for more than a decade, despite research documenting the social nature of the spread and maintenance of drug injecting (Hunt and Chambers, 1976; Johnson et al., 1985).

In the UK during the early part of the 1980s there was controversy over whether supplying clean injecting equipment was an appropriate public health measure, or whether this was encouraging and facilitating a personal problem with addiction. 'Between 1982 and 1986 the Royal Pharmaceutical Society recommended that needles and syringes should only be sold to bona fide patients for therapeutic purposes' (Derricott et al., 1999), although some pharmacists continued to sell syringes. Increasing concerns about HIV led to a reversal of these guidelines along with the opening of pilot needle exchanges in 1986, then an official UK-wide scheme in 1987, with exchanges opening in Edinburgh in 1987 and Glasgow in 1988. Such was the concern and opposition that Glasgow's first needle exchange outside Ruchill Hospital was picketed for about the first six months of its existence, and there were similar difficulties elsewhere.

The community understandably was more willing to pay to avoid becoming infected with HIV – there had been some sensational media scares about discarded needles littering children's play parks etc. – than they were to pay to treat miscreant addicts. Nowadays, the provision of clean injecting equipment is no longer controversial in the UK, with the caveat that the widespread availability of injecting equipment makes it easier to inject and does not constitute a cure or treatment for drug dependence (McKeganey, 2011). However, in the USA, where moral opposition to needle exchanges was stronger and continues, about 9% of drug injectors were HIV positive in 2009 (Wejnert *et al.*, 2012). In Scotland, less than 1% were HIV positive in 2007 (Health Protection Agency *et al.*, 2008), despite there being a high prevalence of drug injecting in Scotland as well as a specific crisis of HIV infection among drug injectors in the early 1980s, particularly in Edinburgh (Robertson, 1987). This huge difference is difficult to attribute entirely to factors other than harm reduction. Only living people can recover from drug dependence.

Unfortunately, clean injecting equipment has been less effective at preventing drug injectors becoming infected with hepatitis, notably hepatitis C for which there is as yet no vaccine. Some 22% of Scottish drug injectors have been diagnosed with hepatitis C and a larger number unknowingly have the virus (McDonald *et al.*, 2010). This is in part because hepatitis is more easily transmitted than the HIV virus and can be passed, for example, by the sharing the filters or water used during injecting.

It is also important to note here that drug injectors are as sexually active as anyone else, and once infected with HIV or hepatitis pose a risk to future sexual partners. Drug injectors can turn to sex work to support their habit, although sex workers tend to be cautious about safe sex when they can (McKeganey and Barnard, 1992b).

Additionally, breaking skin with a needle repeatedly risks contaminating the blood/interior of the body with bacteria that may be present on the skin. This can occasionally lead to serious life-threatening infections such as infective endocarditis, where the heart becomes infected and can be permanently damaged. Another problem can be that lemon juice or vinegar used to acidify heroin can contain fungi that can grow in the eye and cause blindness.

Complex health needs of drug injectors

As well as having problems with dependence, and being prone to well-known infectious diseases, drug injectors also face many other risks to their health due to adulterated drugs, unhygienic injecting practices and a lack of sterile and safe injecting equipment, along with the knowledge and skills to use that equipment appropriately. It is a challenge to inject oneself repeatedly with opiates or other drugs, particularly if they contain insoluble or poisonous material, using syringes without any infection, harm or damage.

People inject opiates (or other drugs) because delivering drugs directly into the blood stream via a vein gives a very rapid effect, and wastes very little of the drug compared to smoking and snorting. The latter becomes a priority as the person's tolerance increases. Most regular drug injectors spend at least £20 per day (retail prices) and need to economise unless they can buy heroin wholesale.

Repeated injecting leaves multiple scars, which makes it increasingly difficult for injectors to find somewhere on their body that they can inject into a vein. Usually, the veins that are easier to self-inject into become scarified first, being the parts of the arms and legs that are easy to reach. Then the choices are to hunt around for a bit of an accessible vein that can be injected into, or move on to harder to reach or riskier places, such as the veins in fingers or toes, the neck, the groin (which risks injecting the artery by mistake) and the penis. Some injectors are also careful to avoid injecting in places where the scars (tracks) easily can be seen by others.

Another difficulty is that injectors use street drugs that may be adulterated with insoluble substances, or may be in preparations that are not really appropriate for injecting. For example, in Scotland, the gel formulation of jellies (temazepam) often block veins and cause tissue damage and abscesses. Yet another difficulty is that injectors may not have access to sterile, appropriate needles and syringes. Generally, injecting with smaller-bore needles is safer, but they can block if the drug solution contains insoluble material.

There are also health issues about the other equipment used for injecting including: the means to clean the injections site; a spoon or something to dissolve the drug in water over heat; the means to clean that spoon; sterile, or at least clean, water; an acidifying agent to facilitate the dissolving of heroin (particularly brown heroin), which ideally should be vitamin C or citric acid; and some form of filter to remove impurities. Ideally, as well as being available, all this should be sterile and not shared with other people.

Heroin injectors are generally well aware of the ideal, but often if it is a choice between foregoing heroin – particularly if they are 'rattling' (withdrawing) – and compromising the ideal, then they will compromise and risk infection and other problems. Even if they are not rattling, intoxication does not help lucid decision-making and best practice. Also, just as domestic kitchens tend to be less hygienic than commercial ones, people are tempted to deviate from best injecting practice when sharing with close friends or life partners. Unfortunately, one's nearest and dearest may be sources of infection.

Another problem is that it is not unusual for a drug injector to have been searching around for a source of heroin, increasingly rattling as they go, so that when they finally get some heroin they are liable to inject it wherever they are, which might be in a car, or outside, without the facilities to be sterile.

Research on addictions

A lot of the people researching and working in addictions in Scotland were social scientists: for example, by 1989 in the west of Scotland alone the mailing list for addiction research was more than 150 people, including seven academic research units at all four universities. This meant that psychological and sociological understandings of drugs and drug problems were relatively influential.

Ideas that began to be developed in the 1980s, which have influenced contemporary policy and practice include:
- addicts have more volitional control over their substance use than is commonly supposed;
- being thought of, and identifying oneself as, an addict affects relationships, including with services;
- the health consequences of heroin injecting can be reduced by psychological and social changes;
- relative deprivation and social exclusion help to cause drug problems;

- heroin injectors often have comorbidities in mental and physical health;
- alcohol and tobacco need to be considered in tackling 'drugs'.

Social science's contribution to policy in the twenty-first century is less about controlling people's behaviour and more about facilitating personal change.

Summary

The story of the heroin epidemic is that it took off very rapidly in the early 1980s. Awareness of it certainly took off quickly and was accelerated by HIV. If the register of addicts is at all an index of opiate use, then it is likely that heroin use prevalence actually increased gradually. Whichever is correct, the large numbers of heroin injectors in urban Scotland in the 1980s caused great concern, but was initially tackled in a piecemeal and ill-resourced manner, using some assumptions that were not particularly helpful, including that heroin might go away again. It was also believed that addicts should be treated only at specialist services and that by and large the solutions were either methadone or abstinence. However, from relatively early on, both public health and social science were also influential in Scotland in developing a more nuanced approach to drug problems that also dealt with drug users and their complex health needs in the community.

CHAPTER 2

They're Dying Like Flies: The Rise of Concern for Problem Drug Users

By the early 1990s there were an estimated 40,000 drug injectors in Scotland (Frisher *et al.*, 1997), mostly in the large cities and their peripheral estates. This chapter will look at how drug treatment practices developed in Scotland, starting with the provision of sterile injecting equipment, looking also at the use of substitute prescribing and considering as well the continued provision of specialised treatment services.

Needle exchanges
Before 1988 Glasgow's drug injectors had benefited from a small number of community pharmacists who were willing to sell injecting equipment to drug injectors (McKeganey and Barnard, 1992a). There had been fewer such pharmacists in Edinburgh (Robertson, 1987). As needle exchanges were opened, the community's understandable fears about them were not realised. People using the exchanges did not hang about outside, break into local flats on the way past or abandon needles in the street. Rather, they quickly made themselves scarce believing that the police were probably watching the exchanges (which they were not). By 1992 there were seven exchanges in Glasgow, and attendance had risen from under 1,000 to 2,800 (Gruer *et al.*, 1993).

In 1985 there had been 166 cases of HIV-infected drug users in Scotland (a number inflated by a backlog of people who had become infected before HIV was widely known); in 1990 there were only thirty-eight new cases; and by 2000 there were only nineteen (ISD Scotland, 2002, Table 38). HIV infection by other routes is a continuing problem, but drug injecting plays a relatively minor part in it.

The containment and control of HIV among drug injectors in Scotland is a major public health success. Before the public health and educational initiatives succeeded, many were pessimistic about the impossibility of getting 'addicts' to change their behaviour; yet they did, which opened people's minds to the idea that perhaps people with drug problems were capable of responsibility.

Substitute prescribing

Substitute prescribing had long been at the discretion of the doctor, leading to considerable variation in the availability of methadone from practice to practice. Some doctors were overwhelmed with patients seeking substitute prescribing, while others refused to get involved. Organised methadone maintenance started in Edinburgh about 1989, with an estimated 1,200 patients by 1994. This involved community GPs prescribing, with some central training and support, as well as a wide enrolment to ensure that no one doctor was burdened with more problem drug users than they were able to manage (Buning, 1994). Glasgow began a similar scheme in 1993, with forty-two GPs prescribing to 729 people. About a year after opening, overwhelmed with demand the scheme had to close temporarily to reconfigure. Difficulties included that staff training had lagged behind demand, and that there was a shortage of staff able to counsel drug injectors along with their methadone.

By 2003 it was estimated that there were just over 18,000 people prescribed methadone in Scotland, of which some 6,500 were in Glasgow and 2,500 were in Lothian, including Edinburgh (ISD Scotland, 2005). One of the quirks of the ways that the NHS gathers statistics is that it is far easier to track prescriptions than people, hence the need to estimate. The number had probably crept up to about 21,000 people as of 2007, but remains an estimate not a head count.

In 1998 drug treatment services recorded 10,010 new attendees, of whom about half said that heroin was their main drug (ISD Scotland, 1998). By 2007 there were 12,222 new attendees (Information Services Edinburgh, 2007). As ever, 96% were of white Scottish ethnicity. Well over half reported using heroin and/or another opiate. About a quarter mentioned benzodiazepines and about the same proportion named cannabis as a drug that was an issue for them. Cocaine and amphetamines were cited less often, and a few people mentioned various other drugs. Cannabis is under-reported, for fewer referred to it than the proportion of users in the general population. Although highly relevant to many people's substance-use problems, alcohol is still absent from these statistics.

The media were inclined to take their traditional pessimistic view of an ever-increasing drugs problem (e.g. BBC News, 2007). This was despite the fact that this looked more like a relatively stable situation over the past ten years, given the difficulties of counting people actually in treatment and other reporting biases, as well as the well-known tendency for better data collection and better service provision to increase the apparent prevalence of things.

If there are approximately 55,000 drug injectors in Scotland (Hay *et al.*, 2009) then maybe third of them are now on methadone. Although methadone is only palliative, it is relatively affordable. To provide sufficiently extended treatment with psychotherapeutic content to 55,000 people would cost hundreds of millions of pounds, which is an order of magnitude larger than our estimate of the current NHS spend on drug problems. Health and social care professionals are broadly pleased with methadone maintenance, despite criticism from some people, including some family and user spokespeople. Substitute prescribing will be discussed further in Chapter 4.

The evolution of drug services
As described in Chapter 1, drug services in Scotland more sprung up then evolved, rather than being formed and developed in a planned way. By the 1990s drug treatment and rehabilitation agencies had become more established and professionalised, and some UK-wide third-sector organisations had set up treatment facilities in Scotland, including Turning Point and Ad-Action. Among those facilities were the first crisis centres. There, people whose drug dependence had led to an acute crisis in their life could be admitted rapidly, in the hope of preventing them from dying of drug-related causes and of getting them to come off drugs. For a heroin injector a 'crisis' means, for example, being stabbed fifteen times and left for dead over drug

debits, or having one's partner die of overdose and losing custody of one's children.

Existing private alcoholism treatment facilities had expanded by then into treating drug addiction, usually with abstinence-oriented twelve-steps methods. Needle exchanges were relatively widespread. Even those adamant for abstinence had come to accept that it was preferable to avoid an AIDS epidemic meantime.

Services had evolved to be of five broad kinds:

- community services, which provided community support for problem drug users and which often had evolved from the social work funded services of the 1980s;
- primary care sector services, which were usually focused on substitute prescribing, but also tried to offer support and counselling, when there was time and opportunity;
- needle exchanges, although primary care and community services often provided sterile equipment too, and needle exchanges tended to take on community support functions,
- rehabilitation services, which provided more intensive interventions aimed at getting people to quit drug use. Rehab services were usually residential, some of these had evolved from services in the 1980s and others had been set up by national third-sector agencies. As discussed in Chapter 1, most rehab services endorsed some form of recovery agenda, but in practice they could be split into services that mostly took referrals from the NHS and other community services, and services that mostly charged private fees directly to the client. The latter private services tended to be strongly Minnesota-model recovery oriented. The services that had a more complex interface with the NHS tended to be less ideological and more tolerant of outcomes other than abstinence, more in line with NHS policy guidelines, such as the first UK-wide guidelines (Department of Health *et al.*, 1991). The guidelines therein are mostly still pertinent today. The most striking change is from the then lukewarm approval for methadone maintenance: 'There is at least a small proportion of patients for whom this is a helpful approach' (ibid., p. 22);

- residential NHS services, which were based on beds in psychiatric hospitals. However, the 1990s saw the dissolution of the big psychiatric hospital as the place where mental health services were located. Where possible psychiatric care occurred in the community, and residential treatment was restricted to people in a mental health crisis. Functionally, this often meant that residential patients had more than one noteworthy psychiatric problem. Problem drug use can be a contributing factor to a mental health crisis: for example, instead of using their medication and being monitored regularly by the mental health team, people may stay chronically intoxicated and chaotic while their mental health symptoms get steadily worse.

During the early 1990s services of all kinds were oriented towards treating the people who became known as 'problem drug users' (PDUs). This slightly euphemistic phrase encompasses the fact that not all such people are 'addicts' and that many of them take mixtures of drugs rather than being dependent on one or two drugs. In Scotland, more PDUs inject than elsewhere, and cocaine and amphetamines are relatively rare. What to do about the majority of drug users who are not PDUs is discussed in Chapter 3.

Funding, staffing and resources
Later on in the 1990s Drug Action Teams (DATs) and Drug and Alcohol Action Teams (DAATs) were set up to co-ordinate policy, funding and service provision regarding drugs across all the sectors who were, or should be, involved including:

- social work;
- education;
- psychiatry/mental health (for the unquestioned ownership of mental health services by psychiatrists began to weaken in the 1990s);
- public health and primary care (which began to meld together during the endless restructuring of the NHS);
- police;
- youth justice;
- probation;

- churches;
- the non-statutory sector (which in many places provided most of the actual drug services).

Typically, much of the funding in an area came from justice, which tended to have most money for anti-drugs work, under the agenda of crime prevention and community safety.

Jumping ahead to DATs gives a quick sense of the potential complexity involved in tackling drugs. Prior to DATs, any mixture of these sectors might fund anti-drug work, or provide anti-drug work. In any given area, it would have been unusual for them all to have involvement, and different sectors often did their own thing. It was not unusual, for example, that different sectors had their own leaflets (no internet yet) and education programmes offering sometimes contradictory information about drugs according to the ideological preferences of the sponsors. To illustrate, a colleague told us of working at Scotland's biggest music festival, T In the Park (which incidentally is sponsored by and uses the logo for Tennents, the most popular lager in Scotland), to hand out health promotion literature about safer injecting. At the next stall they were handing out health promotion literature about preventing HIV, along with condoms. The safer injecting literature was funded in such a way that the Catholic Church had an editorial say in it, so the Church was upset about the provision of condoms along with the (very similar) literature at the next stall; there was clearly a potential for 'confusion'. Our colleague was instructed under no circumstances to place the safer injecting literature into the carrier bag that the HIV stall provided.

Yet the different services tended to be staffed by the same people, who had got into drugs work either by accident, or after taking specialist training. There were relatively few highly skilled and qualified practitioners involved, such as doctors and clinical psychologists. Most drug workers came from nursing, often via mental health nursing, or from social work, or directly via specialist training. Some began as volunteers, often because of prior addiction problems themselves, and developed their skills and training on the job. At entry level, most drug workers either had diploma-level qualifications or had a degree but not in a particularly relevant discipline. They were not well paid, earning about a third of what a psychiatrist who was not yet a consultant earned. Managers in drug services earned a bit more and usually had degree-level qualifications. But there were not many managerial positions. To this day drug services tend to be staffed by relatively low paid and lightly qualified staff. Moreover, the most able staff tend to move up and out of drugs work, because there is only a limited career path within it. This can leave a skills gap.

Drugs workers should be able to:

- conduct assessments for drug problems and ideally mental health problems more widely;
- have good basic counselling skills;
- be able to keep and use complex nowadays mostly computerised records;
- be able to deliver structured evidence-based interventions, such as motivational interviewing or cognitive behavioural therapy;
- have an appropriate knowledge of the local scene.

This is a demanding remit.

Criminal justice

As described in Chapter 1, in the 1980s Scotland began to recognise that a large proportion of offenders were drug users. This has not changed to the present day. From early on there was a widespread feeling that some drug using offenders might offend less should they recover from their drug problems, which suggested that they should be treated rather than prosecuted. Most PDUs were arrested for non-drug offences, and many were repeat offenders, so the police, the procurator fiscal and the courts might know that they were PDUs, might be able to suggest that they sought help, and indicate that getting treatment might benefit their case in court, but no official mechanism existed for referring them to the services that they needed.

However, the main criminal justice response to drugs was to try and reduce supply, by catching and prosecuting drug dealers and drug traffickers, and hopefully seizing large quantities of drugs as well. The media, the public and politicians were all behind the idea of supply reduction. Initially, so was criminal justice, but as the professionals involved got more experienced with drugs many of them became doubtful that supply reduction was a useful activity.

While a minority called for more of the same, until such a time when supply did reduce (and this still goes on), most came to recognise:

- Drug use is demand driven, meaning that when supply can be interrupted the (illegal) market finds ways to reinstate it.
- Drug trafficking and wholesaling are highly profitable and unregulated industries that factor the costs of smuggling, supply seizure, arrest of key suspects and so on into their pricing. It is possible to raise prices temporarily, but impossible to make drug supply permanently unprofitable.
- Despite drug deaths, drug-related violence and other occasional horrors, drug supply is generally a victimless crime that nobody involved complains about, which makes detecting it very difficult except via information received (which may be inaccurate or malicious), or accident.
- At the retail level, 'dealers' tend to be users who are currently in that role to finance their own habit, rather than wickedly dealing in death on purpose.

For these reasons supply reduction is usually ineffective and often unfair (see Naim, 2005; Castells, 1998).

Another problem is still less widely recognised than it should be. It has been a common mistake – fuelled by cinema villains – to fantasise that drug traffickers and other criminals are hierarchically organised (like law enforcement agencies) and should one take out the key leaders of the organisation it will collapse. This may work for organisations based on ideology, because there is not an intrinsic demand for a particular ideology, but it is not effective for illegal demand-driven businesses. Even on the rare occasions when 'Mr Big' is arrested, he is rapidly replaced, and even when huge drug seizures have disrupted local supply this has never lasted longer than a period of months.

The problem of prison

During the 1980s there was a rapid rise in the proportion of Scottish prisoners who were drug users. Cannabis, and other drugs, began to replace tobacco as the informal currency of prison. It seems likely that cannabis in prison had been informally tolerated for a while before then, but imprisoned drug users were increasingly also users of heroin and adjunct drugs. By 2008 prisoners were randomly tested for drugs at reception, and 44% tested positive for cannabis, 38% for benzodiazepines and 34% for opiates (DMIS, 2008).

A large proportion of prisoners use drugs, which poses a fundamental problem that we shall return to for the whole of society in Chapter 3: Is drug use a health problem meaning that drug-using prisoners are entitled to the same health care as they would be on the outside? Or, is drug use a law-and-order issue, meaning that drug use should be punished in prison and prisoners should be prevented from using? The consensus is that drugs are both a health and a law-and-order problem, but fitting the two responses together is particularly awkward in prison.

In the mid-1980s prisons were generally intolerant of drugs, other than perhaps cannabis, and did not necessarily provide the treatments that users might have been receiving outside, including such ameliorative treatment as was available for HIV, and substitute prescribing.

Barlinnie, Scotland's largest prison, experienced a serious riot and siege in 1987. In the aftermath, among other improvements, a conference was held in Barlinnie to discuss drugs in prison, recognising that this was a major problem that might have contributed to the riot. Unusually, prisoners participated in the conference along with staff, researchers and health care professionals. The principal nurse at the time gave a presentation assuring the audience that prisoners received the same medical care in prison as they did outside: for example, if they had been receiving methadone, they would continue to get it, on a reducing dose. During questions, a prisoner simply called him a 'lying bastard', stating that many people did not in reality receive methadone.

In 1993 the World Health Organization (WHO, 1993) published a report recommending that methadone be prescribed in prison, to reduce the spread of HIV, for much opiate use in prison involved the sharing of injecting equipment, often multiple times. Prison also contributed to deaths from overdose, because some people who had used drugs lightly or not at all resumed use on leaving and mistakenly went back to the high doses that they were used to.

Times have changed. In 2008/9 30,850 litres of methadone were prescribed in Scottish prisons (STV, 2010), which amounted to about

617,000 daily doses of 50 ml. This was for an average daily prison population of about 8,000 people that year, of whom we can guess about 30% were opiate users. This would have given every one of them 257 doses in the year. This seems like a lot of prescribing, given that most prisoners are not in prison for 257 days in a year, and that some may not want methadone.

Along with many other improvements to prison life, both staff and prisoners feel that methadone calms and stabilises prison life, reducing the amount of drug-related conflict, violence and debit (Taylor *et al.*, 2006). That it is a sedative drug might also help. By 2008/9 there were also clear guidelines for the management of a wide range of drug problems among prisoners, although there is probably variation in how effectively these are implemented.

By the 2000s the drug-dealing economy in prison was also a large problem (Penfold *et al.*, 2005). Although the quantities of drugs and numbers of users involved are lower than on the outside, the prices are much higher. Consequently, few prisoners can afford to pay for the drugs they are consuming, and it has become common to run up drug debits to be paid on the outside either in real money or in services rendered. This can force ex-prisoners, or family members, into drug dealing or worse to pay debits in prison. The black market in drugs in UK prisons is worth perhaps £22 million per year (*Inside Time*, 2009), although the entire UK market may be worth as much as £4.5 billion. Naturally, these figures are crude estimates at best, and it would be very difficult to tell if methadone, or anything else, had any impact on the scale of the market, or indeed on drug deaths or any other hard indicators of drug problems.

Drug-related deaths

Like most other countries, Scotland conducts autopsies on deaths that are 'sudden and unexpected' and provides reports to the coroner investigating the death and, if appropriate, to the procurator fiscal's office. During 1991 it became apparent that a large number of people in Glasgow were dying of overdose (Hammersley *et al.*, 1995). At that time the autopsy system was oriented primarily towards establishing a cause of death in the individual case. The resultant national statistics could report the number of deaths attributed to specific causes, such as suicide, but the system was not geared up to collate data on the drugs found in corpses' blood, although bloods were routinely screened for a range of common drugs. Therefore, basic questions such as which drugs people were overdosing on were not answered.

There was considerable concern and protest over the probable increase in deaths, with blame attributed either to wicked drug dealers supplying unusually pure heroin or to the lack of consistent methadone prescribing in Glasgow at that time. Consequently, after piloting the monitoring of information about drug-related deaths (Hammersley *et al.*, 1995), a national system for monitoring drug deaths was put in place. As of 2010 about 2.7% of twenty-five to thirty-four year olds died of drug-related causes (General Register of Scotland, 2012), this being the age group most likely to die this way. Since the mid-1990s the number of such deaths has nearly doubled, now being close to 500 per annum. The drugs commonly found were heroin, methadone, diazepam and alcohol. Very few deaths now involve temazepam, because the drug is far less available for abuse. For comparison, the number of alcohol-related deaths in 2010 was 1,318, although there are far more drinkers than heroin users and most of the deaths occur at an older age. Needless to say, it is close to a hundred years since there were any protesters with placards outside Scottish brewers or distillers.

Why did the rate increase, and why is it still so high? There were probably a number of factors. As heroin became widespread in Scotland, the predominant method of use was by injection. This was quite different to the situation in north-east England, or London, where users often smoked, or at least began by smoking. In Scotland, they tended to 'jag' from the start. At the same time, particularly in the west of Scotland, drug injectors from early on also injected buprenorphine – nowadays used as a substitute prescription – and to take temazepam or diazepam along with opiates to intensify the stone experienced. If these benzodiazepines were formulated so that they could be injected, then they often were. Buprenorphine is a long-lasting drug and it is very difficult to overdose on it.

As the years went by, stringent efforts were made to limit the supply of buprenorphine, including a voluntary ban on GPs prescribing it in Glasgow. Buprenorphine is a synthetic drug and was being obtained either by people selling the prescriptions that they had received for pain relief. At the same time, the heroin supply industry in Scotland became increasingly professionalised. Users also began to learn that trying to inject benzodiazepines was often extremely dangerous: for example, injecting the contents of gel-filled capsules caused a lot of abscesses and other tissue damage (Robertson, 1987). There was therefore a gradual switch from the injection of buprenorphine, and benzodiazepines, to the injection of street heroin, with the adjunct oral consumption of large quantities of benzodiazepines. The therapeutic dose of these drugs tends to be 1–2 tablets. Street users were (and still are) habitually consuming 10–20 tablets at a time, and sometimes even more than this if they have built up a substantial tolerance (see Forsyth *et al.*, 2011).

People seem able to take much higher quantities of benzodiazepines orally than by injection. Consequently, a lot of overdoses were associated with heroin/morphine (which are indistinguishable in the blood) and benzodiazepines, and the rise may have been due in part to a gradual switch to a pattern of drug use more likely to lead to overdose, as buprenorphine may have artificially lowered the overdose rate in Glasgow (Hammersley *et al.*, 1995). Another factor is that the Scottish tradition of opiate (and benzodiazepine use) values the 'gouch' – an extremely inebriated and semi-comatose state. As discussed in the Introduction, this may well be an extension of the Scot's traditions of extreme drinking, which can aim more at unconsciousness than merriment. There is not necessarily a big gap between gouching and being sedated to the point of respiratory failure. Another difficulty is that drug injectors can be focused on intoxication rather than pharmaceutical precision and safety. This places them at risk of overdose if they encounter unusually strong heroin, or if their tolerance has gone down after reduced use, for example in prison (Merrall *et al.*, 2010). The initial difference between overdose rates in Glasgow and Edinburgh may also have been due to the relative lack of methadone prescribing in Glasgow.

A final issue, which helps to explain why the rate has stayed high, is that overdose is not always exactly an accident. When overdosers are interviewed in hospital soon after the incident, they report some suicidal ideation (Neale, 2000). This can include seeking to get particularly wasted to obliterate some awful life problem, not caring whether or not they live or die because they feel so bad about themselves, and actually hoping they die, even although they are not precisely trying to kill themselves. It seems plausible that the people who die of overdose will include some who deliberately committed suicide. Within a few days of the overdose, people reconstruct it as an accident and blame the situation or the drugs rather than the way that they were feeling. In the milieu of drug injecting a persona of toughness is needed to avoid exploitation.

So, how should the high overdose rate be interpreted in terms of policy and practice? It seems likely that the rate in part simply reflects the fact that there are a large number of drug injectors in Scotland. Some have expressed concern that methadone is found in an increasing number of deaths (see McKeganey, 2011). However, the data makes it difficult to distinguish a drug simply being present from it helping to cause death, and one would expect somebody taking a prescribed drug to have it present in their body should they die. The initial contrast in the early 1990s between Glasgow, largely without methadone, and Edinburgh, with methadone, was worrying. It is conceivable that without methadone death rates would have risen more steeply.

On the other hand, society is remarkably complacent about deaths related to drug and alcohol use. In contrast, when there were five deaths on funfair rides during 2000, the Health and Safety Executive (HSE) commissioned a major report (Roberts, 2001). To quote the executive summary: 'no deaths or injuries at fairground accidents can be considered acceptable'. There is a one in eighty-three million chance of such a death. At approximately one in a hundred per annum, the acceptable standard for drug injection is shockingly lower. Moreover, the fairground industry is robustly tasked with safety. In negligent contrast, the drugs industry is completely unregulated, while the alcohol industry merely has to put warnings on or near its much more dangerous products, watch its advertising and avoid sales to minors.

Whatever our collective concern about drug and alcohol problems, it does not extend to protecting their consumers in ways that are considered good practice in other leisure industries. Genuine concern about drug users – rather than salacious disapproval of their misbehaviours – remains something of a minority interest.

One promising way to reduce overdose deaths is the Take Home Naloxone training scheme run since 2010 by Scottish Drugs Forum for the Scottish government. Naloxone is an opioid agonist that reverses the effects of opiates, so that a person given naloxone can go from comatose to conscious within minutes, and although the effects are not long-lasting they buy time for an ambulance to arrive. The scheme provides people considered at risk of overdose, and those around them, with a preloaded injection of naloxone for use in emergencies as well as training in overdose management and prevention. This intervention was first mooted in 1998 (Stallard *et al.*, 1998), but it took time to implement because it was necessary for all stakeholders to agree that the ambulance arriving at an overdose should not be accompanied by police officers who searched the premises, followed by social workers who removed any children living there. Not that these things happened routinely, but with local discretion they happened sometimes, which led drug injectors to be reluctant to call emergency services to overdoses.

Medical care of problem drug users

The Department of Health *et al.* (1991) recognised that a patient's problem drug use was relevant in a wide range of health care: for example, high dose drug use interfered with the action of many anaesthetics. At a prevalence of approximately 1%, many medical and surgical services had to learn how to meet the needs of PDUs. This required a major change in stereotyped thinking, away from assuming that drug injectors were uniformly dishonest and unreliable people whose health care needs began and ended with their drug addiction, who were difficult if not downright dangerous patients, whose sole interest in life was getting drugs, and who therefore should only be managed at a specialist service.

There is a common desire in health care provision to treat patients who are responsible for their illness differently from patients who are ill through no fault of their own. This desire is not unique to drug problems. Patients who persist in smoking tobacco, or fail to lose weight, may be denied surgery. Attempted suicides can be treated unkindly in hospital, as are drug overdoses (Neale, 2000). People deemed responsible for their health condition may be denied health insurance.

Against such tendencies, in the 1990s Dr Mary Hepburn established Glasgow Women's Reproductive Health Service (Hepburn, 1998), which initially was designed to facilitate drug-dependent women successfully becoming mothers, ideally, but not necessarily, quitting drug use in the process. In its early days, the service was often told that they were attempting the impossible, yet Hepburn won the *Evening Times* Scottish Woman of the Year award in 2012 for this work, which has evolved into work supporting successful motherhood for vulnerable women more widely. The approach was to work with women, rather than being paternalistic, to see them as vulnerable rather than problematic, and to insist that their right to medical care transcended their drug use, with the welfare of the mother and the infant being paramount.

Hepburn was ahead of her time, but, as PDUs became more familiar in medical practice, staff began to realise that they were not uniform evil stereotypes, but rather vulnerable people often facing severe life difficulties. Although drug injectors can be problematic patients or clients – the 1991 guidelines (Department of Health *et al.*, 1991) mentioned the importance of ensuring that services did not become places where drug injectors congregated – so can people with alcohol problems and other mental health problems. The 1990s saw the beginnings of attempts to consult and engage service users in services and the development of the Care Programme Approach for all clients of specialist mental health services, including PDUs. We return to this in Chapter 4.

Social care of problem drug users

Again, with a relatively high prevalence of people with drug problems, housing departments, social work departments and other services had to develop ways of working with them that did not entail either turning a blind eye or shipping them off to rehab. Housing was one major issue. Few people wanted drug injectors as neighbours.

The problem of the young, single and homeless illustrates some of the challenges (Hammersley and Pearl, 1996). People aged sixteen to eighteen are entitled to lower rates of benefits than older people, a policy to encourage them into further education. Being single, unless they have children, in most areas they lack sufficient points in the housing system easily to be able to get a residence of their own. Sixteen is the age when looked after children in care cease to be the responsibility of the local authority. It is also the age when it is first legally possible for children to leave home without their parents' consent. Consequently, this age group includes people who wish to live independently, after being in care or because their home situation is bad, but they may lack the skills to do so.

Some become homeless because they cannot get accommodation. Those who are housed tend to be placed in rougher areas that require fewer housing points, so neighbours can include other young people and people with drug or alcohol problems. With bad influences, vulnerable young people may end up over-involved in drugs and alcohol and losing their tenancy either because they fail to pay the rent or because they have allowed noisy parties in their home. As these systemic difficulties became recognised, it became possible to develop policies and practices that were more flexible in managing youth homelessness: for example, by providing support to young people recently housed; and by considering the appropriateness of the neighbourhood when housing them.

The chemical generation
Although Scottish drugs policy and practice were, and are, mostly about heroin injecting and other problem drug use, the 1990s saw the rise of another style of drug use that grew along with the dance scene. Initially, raves tended to be unregulated and somewhat anti-alcohol. Dancers took MDMA and a variety of other drugs before, during and after the event (Hammersley *et al.*, 2002). As the years went by, 'going out' became a mainstream activity that occurred in premises licensed for the sale of alcohol, which almost always have public anti-drug policies. Alcohol is the primary drug for going out, but other drugs are commonly involved as well (Aldridge *et al.*, 2011).

A typical session of going out might involve frontloading at home with alcohol, maybe cannabis and perhaps some stimulants, topping up during the event, then coming down with cannabis and sedatives – including alcohol – in the morning. Sedatives might include opiates, but users tended to avoid injecting and would not take opiates on a daily basis. A large minority of younger people used drugs like this, and which drugs were used when was seen as a matter of momentary consumer choice, rather than a lifestyle. This pattern of recreational use has become Scotland's predominant pattern.

As of 2012 it appears that recreational use has influenced the population's attitudes to drugs, which have become less negative, more than it has affected policy or practice. It remains unclear what should be done in terms of services, laws or policies for the majority of drug users who do not fit criminality, vulnerability or psychopathology models. This issue is discussed further in Chapter 4.

CHAPTER 3

The Road to Recovery: Integrating Drug Problems into Scottish Life

This chapter will look at Scottish drugs policy both as an example of the difficulties of reconciling criminal justice and health issues, and as an example of moderately good practice in forming a sensible drugs policy for problem drug use. Unfortunately, before this could happen drug injecting needed to get so widespread that most communities and many extended families included people who were injecting heroin. This slowly switched perception of ownership of the problem, from it being one that belonged to unsavoury criminals in big city housing schemes, to it being a issue that also involved family members, or the families of neighbours, and was not as distinct from heavy drinking as people had initially imagined. It has also mattered that policymakers' families nowadays are among those affected by drug problems.

Yet the injecting of opiates does not typify drug use, moreover the bedrock of drug problems is alcohol. We largely learn about and acquire our attitudes to intoxication from experiences with alcohol. Perhaps ten times as many children in Scotland live with a parent with an alcohol problem (about 100,000) as with a drug problem (perhaps as few as 10,000) (Templeton *et al.*, 2006), although this is going to depend how you define 'problem'. Chapter 4 will look more critically at the continued weakness of policy and practice regarding substance use in general.

The rediscovery of recovery

The Scottish government's 2008 drugs strategy is called *The Road to Recovery* (Scottish Government, 2008). Recovery is a complex and personal thing that Best (2009, p. 12) characterises as being 'about hope, and about self-determination'. He goes on to emphasise that drugs treatment is often not very good, or very honest about its challenges and relative lack of success. For us, it is a major achievement that any country's drugs policy can emphasise PDUs to be the sorts of people who are capable of self-determination as much as anyone else, rather than being viewed as passive receptacles of addictive drugs, or wicked and irresponsible criminals.

There is a long and chequered history to recovery (Yates and Malloch, 2010), but little of it has involved official support. This perhaps changed in 2008, when the Scottish strategy was published and the UK Drug Policy Commission (UKDPC) Recovery Consensus Group (2008) published *A Vision of Recovery*. The latter was a direct response to a rancorous and polarised debate over whether abstinence or substitute prescribing was the 'right' way forwards for the treatment of drug problems. The one sentence vision statement was as follows:

> The process of recovery from problematic substance use is characterised by voluntarily-sustained control over substance use which maximises health and well-being and participation in the rights, roles and responsibilities of society (Drug Policy Commission Recovery Consensus Group, 2008, p. 6).

As the detailed vision states:

> For many people this will require abstinence from the problem substance or all substances, but for others it may mean abstinence supported by prescribed medication or consistently moderate use of some substances (for example, the occasional alcoholic drink) (Drug Policy Commission Recovery Consensus Group, 2008, p. 5).

This attempt at compromise did not bridge the gap between advocates of abstinence as the ultimate legitimate outcome of drug treatment and those with more flexible views of appropriate outcome including the reduction of drug-related harms to the person and the community (McKeganey, 2011). The UKDPC committee consisted of practitioners from the NHS and selected charities, none of whom was from abstinence insistent services, so it was strange to find them enthusing about 'recovery', historically developed by the temperance movement and Alcoholics Anonymous (Yates and Malloch, 2010).

The Scottish Drugs Recovery Consortium (SDRC) is Scotland's central co-ordinating body for recovery work on drug problems. It is an independent charity funded by the Scottish government with an explicit mission to address Scotland's drug strategy. The key messages (SDRC, 2011) are:

- recovery is a journey towards a stable and fulfilling life;
- people can and do recover from drug problems and addiction;
- recovery is a reality;
- recovery is a belief that things can get better and that you are right to be hopeful for the future;
- recovery is contagious.

This particular manifestation of recovery owes more to the twelve-steps-style self-help movements than to current health initiatives such as evidence-based and translational medicine. There is no mention of the talking therapies such as motivational enhancement therapy or cognitive behavioural therapy, which can be effective against substance dependence (Miller and Rollnick, 1991; Beck *et al.*, 1993). However, in Scotland there have rarely been resources to provide such therapies for PDUs to an adequate extent. There is a lack of suitably trained therapists and a lack of therapeutic time to conduct such therapies.

Nonetheless, the recovery agenda at least frames drug problems in a relatively positive light, after the comparatively punitive and criminal justice-oriented responses to the 1980s heroin epidemic (Stevens, 2010). Prior to 2008 it had become relatively widely accepted in Scotland that PDUs deserved treatment rather than punishment, which led to initiatives such as drug treatment and testing orders (see Chapter 4).

There are also some signs that the stigma of drug injecting is reducing. While there is still prejudice against drug users from individuals, it is now accepted that they should receive parity of service from the NHS and other agencies, rather than being discriminated against because their problems are self-inflicted: for example, they can obtain clean injecting equipment and receive vaccinations against hepatitis. It is also accepted that they should be involved in their own care planning and decide what they need themselves.

In day-to-day service operation there are still considerable variations in the reality of the recovery agenda, and there are both overt and subtle pressures for clients and patients to conform to professional requirements or, for instance, lose their substitute prescription. However, this is a delicate area for mental health services in general. Patients have the right to be involved in the planning of their own care, but does this right extend to the right to decline treatment and the right to continue self-destructive behaviours indefinitely? The person-centred philosophies of recovery are not that easy to reconcile with the quite directive and expert-led approach that is common in professional drug treatment. This is not a sideswipe at health and social care professionals, for residential rehabilitation programmes with recovery-oriented philosophies and using peer-support can also be directive.

The issue is complicated by the fact that the recovery word has been taken back by many organisations that do not concord with the principles of rediscovered recovery. If recovery is a personal journey, then methadone might be helpful for one person, but not another. One person might embrace abstinence and the twelve-steps; another might not. One person might find extended psychotherapy useful in addressing the issues that led to a drug problem, while another might find it better to leave drugs behind. Most controversially, some people recovering from alcohol problems find goals other than abstinence helpful for them; others discover that in reality controlled drinking of perhaps no more than two units of alcohol, not very often, soon becomes uncontrolled drinking again. The possibility of controlled drinking can arouse irrational ire among the abstinence-oriented (Sobell and Sobell, 2006). The mirror possibility that some people recovering from drug problems might evolve substance-using practices other than abstinence tends to be considered not only implausible but also unlikely and unethical even to contemplate (McKeganey, 2011). Yet many drug users in recovery continue to make some use of cannabis, of prescribed drugs and, very often, of tobacco. The extent to which they use alcohol varies.

Whatever the difficulties of defining recovery the approach is a welcome change from what went before. As described in Chapter 1, in the 1980s official responses to drug problems tended either to be legal, and often punitive, or to be medical, and often paternalistic.

Bums on seats

As discussed in previous chapters, Scotland has succeeded in preventing an AIDS epidemic spread by drug injecting. It also makes wide use of substitute prescribing, usually of methadone. Taken together, provision of sterile equipment and methadone account for a large proportion of the 'bums on seats' in the NHS's response to drug problems. The relevant policy and practice targets set over the past three decades have tended to focus on numbers of people 'treated' rather than on the success of treatment. The main reasons for this appear to be that:

- without any clients one cannot improve the quality of treatment or assess outcome;
- it is relatively easy to monitor the number of clients who attend services, and generally services now need to count unique clients rather than simply noting the number of visits made by anyone;
- it appears to be widely believed that it is quite difficult to measure the outcomes of interventions to reduce drug dependence.

Outcomes

Actually, to measure intervention outcomes is expensive rather than difficult. It requires following people up some considerable time after treatment, perhaps as long as two years later. This brings the problems not only of waiting for results for longer than the next annual funding round, but also that of locating people two years after they have been treated. The latter issue is intensified for people who are no longer in contact with services as well as those who are completely better, feel no need to maintain contact and may even wish to avoid it to prevent continued stigmatisation. It can also be hard to contact people whose treatment completely failed, who may be disappointed about this and avoid contact or who may have gone completely off the rails into chaos and homelessness.

Measuring outcomes also requires that at the start of treatment the intended outcomes are clear, realistic and agreed. Setting an outcome of zero substance use for all clients means that either the service will fail because that target is too difficult to achieve, or, more commonly, the service will have to fiddle its outcome data to appear to succeed (Miller and Sanchez-Craig, 1996). Setting very weak outcomes is no help either: for example, it is not unusual for services (not just drug services) to assess client condition at the end of treatment by asking them to report their condition using a questionnaire. At that point, clients tend to be grateful to the service and consequently report that they have improved, whether or not they actually have, and whether or not the improvement will be continued. With such light evaluation, almost everything will appear to work, which of course means that services are comparatively judged on other characteristics, such as cost. While cheap ineffective services are better than expensive and ineffective ones, we would prefer effective services at the best possible price.

Another difficulty is that people with drug or alcohol problems of the severity that requires some form of protracted treatment tend to have complex problems, which vary markedly. It is clumsy to expect that every person treated shall achieve, or even aim at, the same outcomes, and some of the desirable outcomes for the person may be nothing to do with their substance use. Again, measuring individual outcomes is possible but it is more expensive than simply auditing the content of urine samples or handing out questionnaires. There is relatively little appetite for high-quality outcome evaluations. Evaluations that also consider treatment processes in order to model the effective components and settings of treatment are even rarer.

Methadone as an example
Lack of evaluation research leads to a dearth of knowledge about what actually works, and why. This, in turn, leads to some peculiar policy and practice guidelines that often lump disparate interventions together under broad headings such as 'substitute prescribing' (with adjunct psychological therapy), and 'psychological interventions'. Any medical committee that published recommendations that 'medicines' be used to treat a medical condition would be a laughing

stock, yet at the bullet point level the guidelines on anti-drug treatment can be nearly as simplistic: an example of the true complexities is that appropriate community treatment of heroin use is 'more than methadone' (Seivewright, 2000). When clients attend for their methadone, then their health status should be monitored and they should also receive psychological therapy to assist them in eventually reducing use of methadone, as well as of street drugs. Moreover, clients often also need help with the practicalities of living a more stable life, notably help with housing. This all sounds easy to implement, but it may not be.

Broadly, there are two ways of prescribing methadone (or buprenorphine) to drug users. One involves the client turning up at a clinic or agency typically weekly to get their take-away methadone supply for the week. The other involves the client coming daily to a clinic or community pharmacy and consuming their methadone there and then. All other things being equal, the latter approach may lead to better outcomes in terms of reduced drug use and other problems (Seivewright, 2000). It is difficult to be clear why this is the case, because from the choice of daily or weekly prescribing flow a whole variety of differences between these two types of service.

Daily on-site methadone involves relatively brief contact with the health care professional providing the methadone, who has probably been trained to ask about how things are going and check for health problems. The health care professional is reasonably likely to be a pharmacist, a GP or a primary care nurse, who has been educated at least to degree level. Specialist psychological therapy will occur separately, if it occurs at all. There is often a shortage of places for local specialist treatment that includes psychological therapy of some kind, so many clients are on methadone and waiting for a treatment place. Consequently, there are likely to be huge individual differences regarding how the daily session is conducted, its content and whether anything resembling psychological treatment occurs. At one extreme, methadone may be dispensed with no more than an exchange of formal pleasantries, while at the other extreme the health care professional and the client may have an excellent working relationship that is therapeutic. Staff training may increase the likelihood of the latter, but from what is known about other types of therapeutic relationship it is likely that better care will be provided when the two people get along well, which is a two-way-street and which probably depends on the extent to which the health care professional is willing and able to be elastic about the timing of sessions.

Weekly take-away methadone involves a longer session with a health care professional. Because the session is longer, it is more expensive for the NHS and takes more, scarce, clinician time. Consequently, the longer session is more likely to be conducted by a practitioner qualified up to diploma level, or with a degree but not in a particularly health- and social care-related subject. Because the session is longer, there is often an expectation that this weekly session should be enough, and the practitioner delivering the session can be expected to prescribe methadone, monitor health, discuss practical issues and deliver psychological therapy. However, the substitute prescription is paramount. At the end of the session the client will usually get their methadone (unless there is some problem), but other components of the intervention may not have happened. If the service becomes more bureaucratic, which is the common trend, then substantial time in the session may become occupied with completing forms about the prescribing process and the welfare of the client, mandatory for service funding.

At worst, in both types of service clients simply get methadone with little or no additional treatment. At the level of broad brush statistics, relatively few people given methadone move on to become entirely abstinent from opiates (McKeganey, 2011). Is this because methadone is useless as an intervention, because it simply replaces one 'addiction' with another, or because methadone without adjunct psychotherapy cannot effect the person changes required for temperance?

Current targets

In Scotland, the emphasis on bums on seats extends to the current targets for drug services, which emphasis doing things quickly:

> By March 2013, 90% of clients will wait no longer than 3 weeks from referral received to appropriate drug treatment that supports their recovery. Waiting times appropriate to alcohol treatment will be defined and incorporated into a target covering both drugs and alcohol by April 2011. As a milestone to deliver 3

weeks from referral to drug or alcohol treatment by 2013/14, by December 2010, 90% of clients referred to drug treatment will receive a date for assessment that falls within 4 weeks of referral received; and 90% of clients will receive a date for treatment that falls within 4 weeks of their care plan being agreed (HEAT, 2010).

Shortening waiting times is always a service user pleaser, but for psychological interventions it ignores evidence that being on a waiting list can itself be a motivating factor for change (Arrindell, 2001). Presumably the expectation of being treated makes people reflect on their lives and begin to implement change. Also, as the sign that used to hang in a university computer room read: 'You can have it, cheap, quick, accurate … Pick any two'. Given the recession, we can be confident that drug services are cheap, requiring them to be quick also will decrease effectiveness: for example, one way of speeding up service appointments is to widen the pool of staff seeing clients. Given there is a national shortage of people with the relevant training and experience, widening the pool usually means diluting the skill level of the counsellors. Alternatively, the same staff may be able to see more people, more quickly, if they reduce the length and number of sessions offered.

What works?
There is quite good evidence about the nature of effective treatment for drug dependence (see Beck *et al.*, 1993; Orford, 2001; Hammersley, 2009; Seivewright, 2000). Despite its importance, there is not space to review this complex area in depth. To summarise, what works:

- involves the basic principles of effective counselling, which include a successful interpersonal relationship between counsellor and client based on warmth, effective communication and mutual positive regard;
- is relatively long-term, across months or years rather than weeks, although residential treatment is not superior to community treatment when they have been compared;
- is flexible and patient in defining recovery, rather than expecting specific outcomes such as abstinence, or absence of offending, within set time scales;

- facilitates change in the client, rather than only paternalistically offering cures, such as detox or substitute prescribing without additional psychotherapy, analysing the past for explanations of problems, or simply letting clients express their feelings;
- focuses on empowering the client to take responsibility for their own recovery and their own management of difficult situations where they are likely to relapse.

Effective treatment tends to address:

- client motivation for change and engagement with treatment;
- the situations and thought processes that lead to and sustain substance use;
- helping the client set achievable goals for treatment;
- reducing the harm of any continued substance use and the related behaviours;
- addressing the client's physical and mental health needs, as well as their addictive behaviours;
- considering and involving family, friends and other sources of social support in treatment as appropriate;
- improving lifestyle and social functioning, which includes modifying offending, antisocial, selfish and irresponsible behaviour.

This is a complex specification that includes much more than simply controlling or ceasing drug use. It is also a high standard for services to achieve with a client group that can be challenging to work with.

The underspend on research and evaluation

In the last thirty years, drug problems have most often been posed as crises that require immediate action. In times of war one does not evaluate the quality of the firearms available and write a report, rather one springs to the front armed with the nearest gun and as much ammunition as possible. At which point we trust the war metaphor collapses. In case it does not, remember the early days of the civil war in Libya in 2011, which clearly demonstrated that the rebel attack without strategy was ineffective. Nonetheless, many times we have heard complaints that money spent on research, evaluation and, indeed, basic record keeping would be better spent 'helping' people. We heartily agree, but unfortunately this supposes that we know how to help. The most vociferous complainers tend to be those most convinced that they have this knowledge. We fear that some of them have sprung to the front armed with broomsticks and fiddles that they have mistaken for rifles.

Given the UK's current financial difficulties, it is likely that budgets for drug services will be cut. Consequently, where services control research and evaluation budgets, these will be reduced further as relative luxuries. For a high-profile problem such as drugs, it is important that the government still be seen as doing something. Nonetheless, relatively brief interventions for serious drug problems are probably ineffective, even if they are offered quickly.

Nationally, the last few years have seen a trend for encouraging research on health-related issues such as drugs involving networks of many different sites and different professions making better use of 'existing data', such as the data routinely collected by services in the course of their practice. On one hand, this is intelligent use of scarce funding and resources. On the other hand, this is a bureaucratic way to avoid funding or doing original creative high-quality research, which tends to be less regimented and more expensive. A typical network of this kind involves six to eight partners in universities and the NHS and attracts funding to the value of less than four standard research grants (approximately under £1 million total). Moreover, considerable resources are required in such networks to keep the network functional and cohesive, before any research is even done at all, eroding the money available for actual research still further. It will be a challenge for any of these networks to find out anything worthwhile, but the 'research' box can be ticked on the 'do something about drugs' list. It also helps that because such a network is focused on existing data it is unlikely to be politically controversial.

Meanwhile, quite a few scientifically uncontroversial ideas remain politically controversial in addiction including that:

- alcohol problems and drug problems are similar and should be tackled together (almost no survey data on both);
- prevention and harm reduction would require acceptance that drug use can occur without problems (the little research on this has attracted official opprobrium);
- cannabis and ecstasy are less dangerous than heroin or alcohol;

- substitute prescribing for drug problems is a palliative not curative treatment.

Scotland's highest-profile research centre on drug problems for the last seventeen years was closed in August 2011, as part of a cost-saving exercise by the University of Glasgow. The webpage (www.gla.ac.uk/departments/drugmisuse; accessed 5 December 2011) refers the reader to 'the University's new Institute of Health and Wellbeing (which) has been established to promote groundbreaking interdisciplinary research across a spectrum of health and well-being subjects'. If one looks at the institute's web pages drugs and alcohol do not figure highly there. This is an interesting change. When the Centre for Drug Misuse Research was established in the 1990s, it was so high profile that it was located in the heart of the campus next to the principal's official residence. Subsequently, it was transferred to a more discrete off-campus location.

Naturally, we welcome health and well-being, but the hard problems of drugs, alcohol, social exclusion and trauma have not gone away. Moreover, we note that accounts of well-being emphasise the transient, mindful, nature of happiness and contentment (e.g. Dalai Lama and Cutler, 2009; Williams *et al.*, 2007), suggesting that it is not humankind's primary natural condition.

In times of hardship, the trend to spend money on glossy research projects rather than useful ones will probably continue. A widespread rule of thumb is that a project should budget about 10% of its overall costs on research and evaluation. From twenty-five years in the field, frequently tendering for evaluation bids, we can state that this is only rarely achieved. We estimate, for example, that expenditure on NHS and other statutory drug and alcohol services in Scotland in 2005 was approximately £50 million, but as far as we can tell nothing like £5 million was spent on research and evaluation.

The gross costs of problem drug use are probably much higher – many billions – but estimates are not reliable because they include the monetarising of intangibles such as the distress caused by crime. Moreover, it may not be appropriate to assign all the costs incurred by PDUs to their drug use, because they often have many other complex and enduring problems. Besides, while the undoubtedly huge costs of problem drug use are routinely used to rationalise action, the expenditure on action has always been comparatively meagre.

It's recovery Jimmy, but not as we know it

Given such difficulties, we suspect that the recovery agenda is partly a cost-saving exercise. If PDUs should be encouraged to self-deter-mine their own pathways to recovery, then this does not need cost very much money. Sometimes, people in recovery choose to work entirely by voluntary mutual support (Yates and Malloch, 2010), which is close to free. Even when funding is offered this will tend to be very modest compared to the funded required by, for example, a team of health care professionals.

Moreover, because rediscovered recovery is often conceptualised as a personal journey, it tends to be holistic, humanistic and spiritual, so those involved in recovery can be wary of scientific generalisations about people and cautious about rejecting or accepting therapeutic practices on the basis of scientific evaluation research. Conveniently for funding bodies, this means that the recovery agenda can, and has, operated largely without any research base at all, although more organised and professional recovery organisations tend to adopt interventions developed in the world of clinical science.

Another difficulty with 'recovery' is that holistic, humanistic principles can extend to accepting all definitions of recovery as valid. Remember that official support for 'recovery' was activated to try and fudge the debate about whether outcomes other than abstinence count as successful treatment, and whether substitute prescribing was a curative treatment, or simply palliative.

Perhaps this debate cannot be fudged (McKeganey, 2011). Indeed we think that there are two versions of recovery, which existed before recent official endorsements of the word. We will call them 'funda-mentalist recovery' and 'liberal recovery'.

Liberal recovery is not easy to capture in a sentence, because it does not have fixed opinions or a fixed approach, but it covers the UKDPC committee on recovery and most professional practitioners and researchers. Liberal recovery tends to be pragmatic and evidence-based, and oriented towards PDUs achieving some form of improvement in their lives, and in their relationship with society.

Fundamentalist recovery is usually abstinence-oriented, often uses Minnesota-model treatment derived from twelve-steps principles, is often residential, often uses peer-support and abstinent ex-users as counsellors, and often makes use of group work as a mainstay of therapy. Fundamentalist recovery also tends to be resistant to evidence because of a strong emphasis on abstinence, at all costs. This emphasis means that clients who are caught using drugs or alcohol are typically discharged and lost to follow-up, leaving a self-selected group of clients who are capable of remaining, or seeming to remain, abstinent for the duration of the programme. Then, because of the emphasis on abstinence, the usual criterion for success is abstinence at the end of the programme. Many fundamentalist services report very high success rates of above 90% at this point (Miller and Sanchez-Craig, 1996) and with the desired result achieved there is rarely further follow-up.

Unfortunately, in outcome evaluation research in mental health it is widely accepted that improvement diminishes with time, so an honest success rate cannot be calculated until twelve or even twenty-four months after treatment. By this time, most drug and alcohol services achieve 20–30% success, and this includes 'fundamentalist' ones on the rare occasions when they have been evaluated in this manner (Allen *et al.*, 1999). But perhaps the concept of 'recovery' itself is mistakenly based on some false assumptions.

False dichotomies
Three false dichotomies have hindered rational responses to drug and alcohol problems. First, that 'drugs' are worse than alcohol and tobacco and are harmful, deviant and unusual activities in society, whereas alcohol and tobacco are widely enjoyed often with little real harm. Second, that drug and alcohol problems belong only to a minority of addicts, leaving a majority of responsible drinkers and perhaps of 'recreational' or 'experimental' drug users. Third, that some 'addictive' drugs – opiates, cocaine products, amphetamines and benzodiazepines – are much more problematic than other drugs, such as alcohol, tobacco, cannabis and ecstasy. Consequently, the 'recovery agenda' in both flavours is primarily about developing, having, then recovering from a serious drug or alcohol problem.

What happens to the much larger and less researched group of people who have health, legal and social problems related to drug or alcohol use, but do not develop dependence and consequently do not experience a dysfunctional and traumatic mental health problem that they need to 'recover' from?

An example of such excessively dichotomised thinking is that Marijuana Users Anonymous was initially set up by marijuana users who felt that their problems were not being taken seriously in Narcotics Anonymous (NA). At NA meetings, cocaine and heroin addicts felt that the marijuana users did not have a proper addiction, should be able just to stop and had not experienced problems on the same scale as cocaine or heroin users.

Scottish policy and practice regarding drugs remains predominantly about the treatment and prevention of problems caused by opiates and cocaine, which are generally conceptualised as being capable of causing addiction independently of the psychological and social conditions of the person. This conceptualisation is probably too narrow and simplistic to drive policy in the future. Indeed, there are clear signs that it is already changing.

Interconnected person-centred practice

There are a number of means in Scotland by which people with drug problems can get the help that they need. The common intent of all of them is to work consistently, with a plan across different agencies that is tailored to the individual and meets their needs, whatever these are, rather than simply focusing on their drug use, their offending, their misbehaviour at school or their homelessness.

Children's hearings

Since 1968 Scotland has operated a system of children's hearings, where children's cases are heard by a panel of three trained lay people, with a professional reporter, in a relatively informal setting (www.childrenspanelscotland.org). Hearings occur when a child has offended, or when they may need to be placed in care. This approach is effective in reducing offending and getting children appropriate help, including with their drug use (Hill *et al.*, 2005). It considerably predates the Youth Offending Teams (YOT) approach that operates in England and Wales. The outcome of a hearing can be whatever mixture of interventions and activities the panel deems appropriate. As with YOT work, an offender does necessarily receive a sentence, but may be required to engage with interventions to address their substance use, their offending and so on.

A specific problem in Scotland is young men mixing alcohol and diazepam then committing very serious violent offences that they often have no memory of afterwards. The result of this is that most incarcerated young offenders have been sentenced for crimes related to violence, often due to alcohol and diazepam mixed together (Forsyth *et al.*, 2011). There are also signs that, as elsewhere, young offenders have been deterred from heroin due to the problems experienced with it by older relatives. Alcohol is nowadays their main drug, but mixed with benzodiazepines it has very unfortunate effects.

Drug treatment and testing orders

Drug Treatment and Testing Orders (DTTOs) were introduced across the UK in 1998, having been used previously in the USA. They were first piloted in England then in Glasgow in 1999, although the first Glasgow DTTO did not occur until 2000 (McIvor *et al.*, 2006). DTTOs were intended for people who were persistent offenders, usually with at least one prison sentence behind them. They were not perceived as some easy way of escaping punishment, but as a last resort after repeated punishment clearly had failed to change behaviour.

A DTTO involves the person being required to undergo drug treatment and to have urine samples tested repeatedly, usually monthly, throughout the period of the order. Progress and compliance are monitored by the court, usually in sessions that are less ritualised than full court: for example, the judge may not wear robes. Drug treatment may be any combination of interventions, depending on the individual. Most often it involves some form of rehab.

More recently, DTTOs have been piloted also for people who have less extended careers of drugs and crime, with the objective of helping them before they develop more serious problems (McCoard *et al.*, 2010). There is evidence that DTTOs reduce offending and drug use and that coerced treatment is not generally less effective than voluntary treatment (McCoard *et al.*, 2010; McIvor *et al.*, 2006).

The care programme approach

The Mental Health National Service Framework of 1999 introduced the concept of a care programme for all patients of specialist mental health services (see Department of Health, 2008), which would include drug users attending NHS mental health services. Nowadays, these might be based in former psychiatric hospitals, but more often are located in the community and may be part of the local primary care trust. As discussed in previous chapters, many drug services are not NHS services, although they take referrals from the NHS, but nonetheless the care programme approach seems like a good idea in general, and any service that engages with the NHS should be using it.

Its key concepts are straightforward to state but trickier to implement. Each patient or client should have a care programme that has been agreed by them, and by all the services that they are likely to be involved with. They should also have a key worker who is responsible for the care programme, which should be in a form that is available to all services at all times. The programme should be based on an assessment of the client and include not only a diagnosis of their mental health problems but also their mental, physical and social condition and their health, mental health and social care needs. It should assess client strengths as well as weaknesses.

Such an approach (Department of Health, 2008) views the client as a person first and service user second; it puts the individual client at the centre of the plan, sees them in the round, is respectful towards them, builds their confidence and encourages mutual respect. Clients should care for themselves wherever possible, while their lay carers are also important and have needs too. The care programme is subject to regular review.

Key principles

These initiatives share common principles. They:
- try to get all services and the client to use a common approach;
- focus on the person in the round, rather than just on a diagnosis or presenting problem;
- expect the person to play a central role in planning and implementing;

- work on the person's needs and strengths, rather than just treating their more obvious weaknesses;
- consider the social and psychological context of the person's problems.

Moreover, there is recognition that the severity of a drug problem for the person can vary as a function of other factors in their lives.

Of course none of this happens perfectly all the time, but it is a great improvement on the days when services barely communicated and when a diagnosis of drug dependence usually led to a prescription, or a hasty referral to a specialist service, which typically offered a treatment to get the person off drugs and, if that did not work, then the client was more or less back where they had started.

Illegal leisure

As well as society getting used to the presence and problems of heroin and drug injecting, it has also become much more used to the general presence of illegal drugs. After the rise of the dance scene and ecstasy, the licensed drinks trade recaptured the market and nowadays 'going out' usually occurs primarily in licensed premises, which invariably have a 'no drugs' policy, which is enforced more or less rigorously. Going out involves a whole evening and can extend most of the night. It can mean getting ready at home with friends, going to a pub, having a meal, perhaps moving on to a music gig or other event, going to a club where there is dancing and sometimes other entertainment and, when the club closes, going back to someone's home to chill out and wind up the night. The whole experience can last ten hours or more (say 6 p.m. to 4 a.m.). With phones, Facebook and instant messaging, planning the night and meeting up with friends is a much more fluid process than it used to be, with the result that commonly people meet up with people that they did not plan to see.

Drinking occurs throughout the night, starting at home. Even quite modest consumption per hour leads to heavy intake over the night and may be one cause of the high alcohol intake in the UK (Hammersley and Ditton, 2005). People also take other drugs, including cannabis before and after, rather than while out, because it is easily detected in licensed premises. Stimulants such as cocaine or amphetamine, MDMA or mephedrone are used to enhance dancing and sociability, and sedatives such as benzodiazepines or opiates to come down afterwards. It is feasible to smuggle pills or powders into licensed premises, even if customers are searched. Some premises tolerate cocaine and may even have washrooms with ideal surfaces for cutting and snorting it (or indeed any powdered drug). Consequently, someone going out is liable to encounter drugs and intoxicated people, even if they have taken little or nothing themselves.

Because of this and other exposure, drugs have normalised (Aldridge *et al.*, 2011) and are seen as part and parcel of certain types of leisure, even by non-users and ex-users. Many people largely grow out of drugs, as they acquire roles and responsibilities that make all-night partying more difficult to fit in. Most people manage drug use without becoming drug dependent. Approximately 1.5% of Scots over sixteen are PDUs (assuming about 60,000 of them), but 7.2% report having used an illegal drug in the past year (MacLeod and Page, 2011), meaning that 80% of current users are not PDUs. As these figures are for adults, it is implausible that most are new users or experimenters, although some may develop drug problems later. There is a need for further research and understanding of the difference between a heavy drug user and someone who becomes drug dependent (Hammersley, 2011; 2012). It is also essential to understand forms of drug problems other than drug dependence: for example, the violent young offenders mentioned above might not have met criteria for dependence on alcohol, or diazepam, but the combination nonetheless poses a serious problem.

It should be important to find out how normalisation has affected problem drug use, but there is no such research. Has more familiarity with drugs led to more informed consumers who can avoid heroin or who use it cautiously without developing dependence? Or, as is the common assumption, does an increased prevalence of all drugs lead to an increased prevalence of PDUs? Or is normalised drug use irrelevant to problem drug use, which is more about deadening and escaping from major life problems and psychological pain?

CHAPTER 4

If Not Repression, Then What?

A major dilemma for drug policy is deciding the extent to which drug use and drug problems are health issues or those of civil order and criminal justice. Most countries have struggled with drug use and drug problems by adopting a melange of health and legal responses that have rarely fit well together or achieve the desired outcomes of reducing drug use and/or drug problems, including related crime. Until very recently, it was commonly argued that there was no alternative to banning drugs. However, calls for change, particularly for cannabis, are increasing (see Transform – www.tdpf.org.uk; and Drug Policy Alliance – www.drugpolicy.org). This chapter will propose that the history of tobacco and alcohol shows that society eventually accommodates drugs known to be harmful and that there are some advantages to this, including being able to take a more compassionate approach to the issues.

During the 1980s most politicians appeared to believe that it would be possible to limit the supply of heroin and cocaine – which were the main drugs of concern – while sitting on the fence regarding cannabis. Since then, nobody has faced up to the scale of the drugs industry, even though the USA spent $7.2 billion on supply reduction work in 2004 from a total of $11.7 billion on drugs work of all kinds (Executive Office of the President of the USA, 2004), which is by far the largest expenditure globally. Nonetheless, the illicit drugs industry may be the world's largest industry (Castells, 1998), being worth at least $45 billion, and it is guessed as much as $280 billion (Thoumi, 2005). In a true war victory tends to go to the side with best resources (Smith, 2006), by which measure the drug suppliers are winning by a good margin, despite the somewhat self-serving optimism of those concerned with supply reduction, who still report that *eventually* they could win – given more power and resources of course. For example, the global area visibly cultivated by opium poppies in satellite photographs has decreased (United Nations Office on Drugs and Crime, 2006), although this could be due to many factors other than the success of international law enforcement, including the increased diversification of the products called 'drugs'.

As discussed in Chapter 1, repression works better when there is not mass demand for the drugs being controlled. The British model appeared to work well because relatively few people in the UK were opiate users. The model was unable to accommodate the huge rise in opiate use by unemployed urban youth in the 1980s and never offered any solution to the use of other drugs such as cannabis, ecstasy or other drugs commonly used for fun, without dependence.

Drugs as a moral problem

Perhaps drug use and drug problems are not intrinsically health issues at all, but merely problems of morality (Szasz, 1974). This form of argument can be used to support either the deliberate repression of some forms of drug use that society considers immoral, or the depenalisation of most forms of drug use, on the basis that many drugs are no more immoral or harmful than alcohol or tobacco. Were it so simple.

Repression is often held to be justified because of the truly awful health problems associated with problem drug use. Are these health problems truly due to the chemical ravages of specific drugs, or do current drugs laws and policies actually make things worse?

Focusing only on the injection of heroin and its adjunct drugs, as has long been known (Szasz, 1974), many of the resultant health and social problems stem from having to buy impure heroin of unpredictable strength, that often contains insoluble matter, at a very high price, then inject it under conditions that are not always sterile. These problems are made worse by society's general revulsion at heroin injecting and the stigmatisation of heroin users as evil, criminal, untrustworthy people whose problems are entirely self-inflicted, and who therefore deserve what they get.

Stigmatisation affects the funding and provision of services for heroin injectors. As described in previous chapters, these tend to be underfunded, and can sometimes be provided in a grudging or dogmatic way, where treatment is given only to people who can prove that they 'deserve' it by keeping off street drugs, or by abstinence. Stigmatisation and illegality abolish any hope of managing the behaviour of the drugs industry. The people involved in supplying and selling drugs are free to behave as responsibly or irresponsibly as is expedient at the time.

The urge to repress drugs taps into common human desires to construct 'risk' as a moral issue (Douglas and Wildavsky, 1983), condemn the behaviour of others and to punish transgressions (Hammersley, 2009).

Media, law, politics, science

Quis custodiet ipsos custodes? (Juvenal, *Satire VI*, lines 347–8)

Strictly speaking, one would expect that the legal dimension of drugs policy would be closely informed by science, just as it is regarding the control of infectious disease. However, morality also plays an implicit role (albeit largely unacknowledged and reflecting the personal religious and moral values of the lawmakers). This situation clearly causes problems, and the fact that Scotland has quite a distinct legal system only serves to add to these. And into this heady mix we must add two further confounders: the sometimes vague way in which legislation is written; and how it is then interpreted and implemented.

On several occasions in the 1990s, for example, we were told in private by senior civil servants that the UK could not change cannabis laws without being in violation of key international treaties. The governmental opinion was that the Netherlands approach of tolerating cannabis and cannabis cafes in the cities for the greater good was on dodgy ground in terms of international law. Since then, various other governments have changed laws in the direction of depenalising some drugs, apparently without falling foul of international law. Moreover, the UK has reduced the severity of the classification of cannabis, then increased it again. It is not only at the international level that people do not necessarily agree about the law.

It needs to be borne in mind that most politicians do not really know what they are talking about when it comes to 'drugs'. They know what they know mainly via the same conduit as most other people – that is, the media. Alternatively, politicians are briefed by administrators or civil servants who gather their information via the media. Nowadays, the accessible media includes a mass of scientific research, but being able to search, interpret and handle 'the literature' is a highly developed specialist skill, which tends to require a lot of prior knowledge that civil servants, politicians and journalists usually lack. Even academics flounder to interpret the literature outside their specialist area.

What we have, therefore, is a symbiotic and unhealthy relationship between media and politics, in which the media produce an amalgam of truth, half-truth, untruth and speculation (constructed with their own ends in mind: namely to sell advertising space). This in turn is repeated by politicians, giving it further credibility when it is re-presented by the media. None of this is to suggest in any way that politicians are deliberately lying, but what they are doing is providing wholly undeserved credibility to the media, and allowing them in turn to re-present their mix of truth, half-truth, untruth, speculation, anecdote and so on as reality. Over the years, for example, politicians have repeatedly rejected widely known truths, such as that cannabis is not very harmful, as incorrect and sending the wrong sort of message.

Scientific understandings can gain entry to this shared reality, but rarely by stating that it is incorrect. Scientists entering media reality can require them to simplify their knowledge to the point of banality, or to promote 'cures' and 'dangers' prematurely. In the black-and-white terms of the media:

- heroin is evil (never mind that medical use of opiates for pain far surpasses their abuse for pleasure);
- mephedrone is dangerous (never mind that there is a low prevalence of morbidity and mortality, and the drug may not be implicated in the problems noted);
- a 'cure' for addiction has been discovered.

Even more worryingly, when scientists decline to enter the media world due to a lack of scientific evidence, the media happily projects, speculates or simply invents the facts. Scientists tend to be fond of the phrases 'it is complicated' and 'it depends what you mean', which are anathema to politicians and the media.

One improvement over the past forty years has been wider recognition that drugs are here to stay and that the problems are complex, rather than that they are a crisis that must be acted on with or without adequate knowledge. Nonetheless, addiction science and the common media portrayal of drugs have very little in common. One is a complex set of issues; the other is a source of popular stories.

The following quote illustrates extreme circular reasoning:

> A number of years ago, I was actually introduced to someone in the DEA [Drug Enforcement Agency] at a conference somewhere. As I'd never actually met a real 'Narc' before, I decided to cut to the chase and see if a straight question would get a straight answer. The conversation, such as it was, went something like this:
>
> John Dee: 'What is the problem with drugs then?'
>
> DEA: 'They're against the law.'
>
> JD: 'Yes, I get that bit, but why are they against the law?'
>
> DEA: 'Because they're bad.'
>
> JD: 'Yes, yes, but what I'm trying to get to is *why* are they bad?'
>
> DEA: 'Because the law says they are.'

And so on (Dee, 2007).

Most media and political conceptions of drugs tramp a larger circle than this, but circular reasoning is still present. For instance: there is a new 'drug'. It is a drug, therefore it is probably dangerous, so every instance where it seems to be harmful is reported to protect and warn the public; this enhances public concern and the prevalence of use, which in turn increases the raw number of cases of risk/harm. Therefore, the drug is banned, which leads to a further increase in use (because if a drug is dangerous it is also strong and interesting), no control over the quality or conditions of its supply and gangsters dealing in it. Then there really are some problems, confirming that the drug was dangerous all along.

The desire for intoxication is irrepressible

To our knowledge, the only cultures that do not use intoxicants are those that have literally no access to them, because of the rare situation that intoxicants cannot be obtained or manufactured locally and the culture has no access to trade. One example is the Inuit cultures of the Arctic. Unfortunately, as with native cultures across North America, when alcohol was introduced in trade it soon became desired and caused problems.

Most global religions sensibly consider habitual intoxication as a barrier to virtue, wisdom and piety (including those that use drugs in sacrament), but different cultures vary in the extent to which lapses from ideal moral standards are tolerated and forgiven. Religious statements, usually about alcohol, can be taken literally, but need not be. Most statements predate modern chemistry so do not explicitly mention most of the drugs now available. It is hard to find societies where people are more abstemious in private than they claim in public. In many societies wealthy people consume illegal drugs – whether that is alcohol is Saudi Arabia, or cocaine in the City of London – and little or no attention is paid to drugs grown and consumed locally by peasants, even if the same drugs constitute a problem elsewhere.

Moreover, during the twentieth century the question of what should be banned became much more complex. The following list shows when some key drugs, which are currently in widespread use, are first known to have been used, or were first invented or discovered:

- alcohol (fermentation) 10,000 BC;
- tobacco (growing) 6,000 BC;
- wine 5,000 BC;
- opium 4,500 BC;
- cannabis 3,000 BC;
- tea 2,737 BC;
- tobacco (evidence of use) 100 BC;
- distilled spirits 800 AD;
- coca leaves 1000 AD;
- coffee 1600 AD;

Since the development of modern chemistry there has been:

- cocaine 1855;
- heroin 1874;

- amphetamine 1877;
- MDMA 1912;
- LSD 1938;
- methadone 1939;
- diazepam 1960;
- cannabinoids 1980s;
- mephedrone 2007.

Of the ten drugs that existed before 1800, only tea/coffee and coca leaves appear to be relatively harmless. Setting them aside, during most of human history globally traded inebriants were limited to alcohol, opium, cannabis and tobacco. Substantial and repeated moral and scientific concerns about these have not inhibited their widespread and persistent use.

Tobacco as a case study

A legal drug makes a useful comparator with illegal drugs, because much more of its history is documented. Cigarettes became legal and very widely used although: they were initially banned and subject to harsh sanctions; health problems were known (and lurid social problems imagined); the tobacco industry has been motivated by profit rather than the consumers' best interests; and the industry has been involved in sometimes shady, even immoral, activities. Consequently, some widely held arguments against depenalising and regulating illegal drugs become rather weak. These include that:

- drugs are harmful – so is tobacco;
- the difference is we did not know the harms of tobacco and alcohol when permitting them – we did;
- drug traffickers are wicked – the tobacco industry has done some bad things.

From its discovery by Europeans in America and introduction to Europe in the sixteenth century, tobacco use spread rapidly in Europe, then elsewhere, despite concern, opposition and repression in places (CNN, 2000). The tobacco industry became commercially important and has remained so. Tobacco also spread smoking as a feasible and acceptable form of ingestion, later applied to other drugs. Cigarettes became rapidly popularised only after the invention of an automated rolling machine in 1883 allowed their mass-production, and their spread was helped by the First World War, which distributed cigarettes widely to forces and civilians alike as a convenient and classless form of tobacco use (CNN, 2000). As early as 1900, 4.4 billion cigarettes were sold in the USA, and some 73 billion by 1923. This was despite substantial opposition: for example, in 1901 only two of the forty-five US states were neither considering nor had passed anti-cigarette laws. Claims about cigarettes echoed modern warnings about drugs: for example, one Tennessee judge said: 'There are many [cigarettes] whose tobacco has been mixed with opium or some other drug, and whose wrapper has been saturated in a solution of arsenic' (Borio, 2003). By 1909 fifteen states had banned cigarettes entirely, but in 1927 Kansas was the last to repeal the ban. Lung cancer rates had already trebled.

Nonetheless, cigarettes became increasingly popular because they were easy to mass-produce, hence cheap and convenient to smoke. Cigarettes were much more widely used by women, who had previously generally used snuff or nothing, but had come to find cigars and pipes unladylike. Since the First World War, mass cigarette smoking has been the principal form of tobacco use and it has gradually displaced other forms of use worldwide.

Problems were known all along

The adverse health and social consequences of smoking were recognised from the start. In the seventeenth century punishments for tobacco supply included having hot lead poured down the throat; for first use, punishments included execution or, more leniently, whipping, a slit nose and transportation. In France tobacco could be sold only on prescription (Borio, 2003, Chapter 3). By the mid-nineteenth century the medical effects of tobacco were suspected, and its effects on cancer were first documented statistically in 1939 (Borio, 2003, Chapters 4 and 5), although the size and severity of the links between cigarette smoking, lung cancer and cardiovascular diseases were not fully accepted until the 1960s. Meantime, cigarette smoking came to be regarded as a vice that could be beneficial to manage people's 'nerves' and concentration. It is surprising from 2012 to look back at an era when cigarette smoking occurred everywhere including buses, trains, pubs, restaurants, offices, seminars, cinemas, hospitals and people's homes. Whatever drug epidemic has hit us since 1960, drugs – tobacco being a drug – are no longer as widely and openly used as they used to be.

The tobacco industry knew from early on that cigarette smoking was harmful and did its best to conceal this information, as well as concealing how highly dependence-forming tobacco was. Meanwhile it developed strategies for managing the fact that the number of smokers was going to decrease as the news got out (see Ling and Glantz, 2002; Feldman and Bayer, 2004).

The industry has resisted accepting any responsibility for the damaged health of tobacco users, although it has now been successfully sued for compensation by smokers, health insurers and governments (Barbera, 2000). The industry line prior to 2000 was that smoking is an individual choice. The alternative view is that the health damage caused by tobacco and the sometimes very severe difficulties of stopping smoking make it a product that is dangerous and unsuitable as something to take for pleasure, relaxation or concentration.

The history of the cigarette is very consumer-driven. Mass cigarette smoking developed because there was a large demand for the product, despite bans, much opposition and awareness of the health problems. The industry met the demand, but they did not create it. Once cigarettes were established as a mass habit, the known health risks were neglected to the point that it was necessary to demonstrate decisively that cigarette smoking caused cancer and cardiovascular disease, then pursue the point forcefully. The basic facts had not changed across the twentieth century, but their use and appreciation changed markedly and medicine made smoking a priority once the extent of the excess mortality due to smoking was incontrovertibly established.

The tobacco industry is a large one with a lot of political influence, particularly in the USA, which is a major producer. Among the many American political figures related to or otherwise linked to the tobacco industry was Harry Anslinger, the head of the Federal Bureau on Narcotics, who was married into a tobacco family. Margaret Thatcher went from being UK prime minister to being a 'geopolitical consultant' for Philip Morris at $250,000 per annum plus $250,000 contribution to her Foundation (Wikipedia, 2012). In the USA, the tobacco industry makes substantial contributions to political funds, and the Bush administrations were linked with tobacco in a number of ways (Dreyfuss, 1999).

There have been accusations that the tobacco industry has been involved in tobacco smuggling, and in other related illegal activity including money laundering, bribery and even links to terrorism. The Action on Smoking and Health (ASH) website (www.ash.org. uk; accessed 2 June 2007) contains documents and links showing this problem and those described below.

In the twentieth century more people died of smoking-related disease than died in the First and Second World Wars combined. Although anti-smoking activities have reduced tobacco smoking in Scotland and many other developed countries, smoking is still globalising and the total market has not yet shrunk. The WHO predicts that more people will die of smoking-related causes this century than in the twentieth century, despite anti-smoking interventions (Mackay and Eriksen, 2002).

All this suggests that it is extremely difficult to get rid of any drug once it has got established as a desirable psychoactive one that can be taken for pleasure. Beyond some critical level, consumer demand is sufficient to motivate continued supply if the profits are high enough, even in the face of extreme repression and strong legal sanctions. Moreover, the globalisation of supply means that demand among a small minority of consumers, in many places, is enough to turn a very good profit. This applies whether the industry is legal, or illegal. It even applies when the drug is incontrovertibly harmful to health.

Repression is ineffective and unworkable

Consumer demand persists in the face of repression: for example, in Saudi Arabia alcohol use is illegal and only occurs in specific private settings. Use and supply are taken very seriously as problems, and severe legal sanctions can be applied such as flogging and imprisonment. In consequence, alcohol use in Saudi Arabia is a more extreme behaviour than in Scotland: rather like opiates in the days of the British model, it tends to be covert and restricted to wealthy people, foreign workers and some deviants (see for example, Kelso, 2002; Hiro, 2001).

This is an interesting example because, the conventional myth goes, some drugs such as opiates are so addictive that naturally their users would risk flogging to take them, while, in contrast, alcohol is supposedly a largely harmless inebriant when used in a temperate and responsible manner. Do people risk flogging for a mere lifestyle accessory? Or are most foreign workers in Saudi Arabia alcoholics? Indeed, where alcohol is illegal, there are fewer social norms governing use, which may lead to more extreme use. The world does not divide conveniently into addicts and normal users, or into addictive and non-addictive drugs.

Controlling medicines, such as the opiates and benzodiazepines, is also morally problematic. Does temperance apply to medicines? Presumably it is acceptable to use diazepam as a medicine to aid sleep or reduce anxiety, but it is not acceptable to take it to get inebriated. Is it admissible to use marijuana as a medicine, even though it is more widely used as an inebriant? What if you get a bit intoxicated? Is this a problem – after all, many medicines 'may cause drowsiness' (which drug users robbing pharmacists use to decide whether the tablets are worth stealing). Even back in the nineteenth century, 'patient medicines', which tended to contain alcohol and perhaps opium or cannabis, were consumed by many teetotallers.

As discussed in Chapter 2, many heroin injectors use heroin in part for pain relief, both physical and psychological. Given that pain is a highly subjective experience and there is no way of objectively diagnosing a person's pain without relying on their self-report, why does the say-so of a doctor make a fundamental moral difference? Cases such as Michael Jackson suggest that perhaps it does not.

Can a sophisticated global industry be repressed?

Globalisation of supply means that controlling products easily made from plant materials is very difficult. There has also been a recent rise in the sale of 'legal highs' based on molecules that are chemically similar to controlled drugs. As has become a common trend (Ericson, 2006) some have been banned merely in case they should be harmful, because they are similar to other banned drugs, or because they have been associated, however tenuously, with misadventures. Which ones are banned varies from place to place, illustrating the difficulties faced by national and state lawmakers trying to catch up with a global consumer industry. Banning some molecules as potentially harmful risks the sale of others, perhaps eventually including really harmful ones (Hammersley, 2010). It is probably impossible to ban every molecule that has psychoactive effects, and, even if this were a good idea, consumers could always turn to inhaling widely available solvents, including petrol and other toxic ones, which is what people do if no other inebriants are available to them (see www.re-solv.org).

As with many technological progressions, the rate of introduction of new drugs has speeded up over time, accelerated more with the development of modern science, and it shows signs of expanding yet more. The schedule of controlled drugs lists thousands of chemicals, most invented since 1900. Moreover, the rate of diffusion of new drugs is now extremely rapid. Mephedrone had become available around the world by 2010, three years after it seems first to have been manufactured.

The nature of drug trafficking has changed to be more about the efficient production, processing and distribution of illegal substances, and less about the specific drug involved (Naim, 2005). The 'legal' highs industry operates in parallel with it. Currently, legal highs are possibly inferior equivalents of banned substances, so when a legal high is banned there is little demand for it on the black market. However, there are already exceptions to this such as products containing synthetic cannabinoids that can be more potent than natural ones (Funada, 2010).

While 150 years ago it was perhaps feasible to ban and successfully repress a specific drug for which there was little or no local demand, attempts to repress nowadays are faced with a complex, evolving world of drug use in which, as some drugs are banned, others are developed or popularised and where the boundaries between medicine, inebriation and intoxication are often unclear. Moreover, drug issues have globalised, so that almost everyone has some awareness of other drugs and practices via the media, tourism and migration.

Nothing any longer is unquestionably good – in the sense that everyone does it without the slightest doubt – or totally bad – in the sense that nobody does it because it does not even occur to them. Modern choices of inebriant are more about social and personal identity, rather than being unquestioned cultural imperatives. This applies both to people, such as many in the UK, who use a variety of different substances on varying occasions and to people who have made specific choices based on religion and morality. Similarly, nowadays it is necessary to decide the extent of one's tolerance or intolerance of the drug-using practices of others, because it is impossible to inhabit a society where drug practices are uniform and always to your liking: for example, the complications of being a Scottish Muslim include that Scottish nightlife centres on going out in places where alcohol is drunk and drugs may be taken. Repression can also stimulate substance use: for example, apparently there is a growing alcohol problem in Iran, with drinking occurring in part as a rebellion against the strict religious state.

Nowadays, inebriation has joined a long list of human activities that receive widespread moral condemnation, even from people who sometimes do them: for example, extra-marital sex; sex with relatives; killing people; hitting people; cruelty to people; lying, cheating, stealing; and charging exorbitant interest on loans. Policy and practice need to work with a world where people often disapprove of inebriation, yet indulge in it. Broadly there are three options:

- Ban all harmful drugs, including alcohol and tobacco. This is morally logical, but criminalising the alcohol and tobacco industries seems unlikely to improve things and, given whisky's central place in the marketing of Scotland, seems politically implausible.

- Legalise everything for which there is mass demand, with the practicalities to be decided, such as who would sell heroin if it were legal to do so and at what age consumption would be legal. Despite its attractiveness as a sound bite, 'legalisation' is rather meaningless, for drugs are heavily regulated even when they are 'legal' and it seems unlikely, for instance, that corner shops would be allowed to sell heroin to children.

- Regulate drugs in appropriate ways. This is what actually happens already, once one counts alcohol and tobacco as drugs. However, to extend regulation to currently illegal drugs requires a conceptual shift from thinking of drugs as crime, to thinking of them as issues of health and safety

– that is, drugs should generally be made available in some forms under some conditions, unless they are truly poisonous (we are not free to buy and drink methanol). Then use the law to minimise harms. This has happened in the past with cigarettes, alcohol, tea and coffee (Standage, 2007), so it is conceivable that it will occur also for some drugs. However, until drugs policy becomes more rational, this is unlikely.

CHAPTER 5

Developing a Rational Response to Drugs

Over the years discussed in this book drug problems were frequently described using extreme metaphors (Ditton and Hammersley, 1996), included military ones depicting drug problems as so serious that they needed to be fought in a 'war' with the police, customs and courts on the side of good and 'dealers in death' on the side of evil. As in many real wars, the enemy was depicted as so dehumanised and immoral as to justify any methods to combat them, including ones that violated civil rights, involved disproportionate sentences and sometimes included law-enforcement tactics of dubious ethicality, such as seizing people's assets without having to prove that they were the profits of drug trafficking.

Another popular set of metaphors were the maritime, which entailed describing how 'tides', 'floods' and 'waves' of drugs, or drug-related violence, or drug-related crime, were sweeping the country. Maritime metaphors imply a force of nature that washes over a country without the control or agency of individual people. With hindsight, this is rather an odd way of depicting a personal vice, the habit of which is passed from person to person.

The most persistent set of metaphors depict drug dependence or addiction as some sort of disease. Here, we are going to use the term 'addiction' to refer to the looser and more everyday understanding of this issue and 'dependence' to refer to a more tightly evidence-based scientific definition: for example, people can be addicted to food, cannabis, exercise and sugar, but the evidence is that they are not usually dependent on them. All dependent people are addicts, but not all addicts are genuinely dependent by any careful and rigorous criteria. Consequently, it cannot be true that all 'addicts' have a disease, even if they have difficulties controlling aspects of their behaviour. Is dependence a disease?

If dependence is merely a disease in the sense that it would benefit from the attention of health care professionals and health sciences, then this is an uncontentious tautology. Dependence is clearly a behavioural or mental health problem that has real effects, which are problematic and not entirely dependent on how society views and judges it. Opiate dependence can include: going to extraordinary, sometimes bizarre and often illegal lengths to get opiates; taking risks that appear excessive, such as risking serious tissue damage or even death by injecting in dangerous places such as the groin; and the continuing use of opiates notwithstanding dreadful problems related to its use. Alcohol dependence is not much different.

However, the disease metaphor has more commonly presented drugs as a plague that is having such tragic effects that all efforts must be exerted to stop it. Reactions to the real plague were similar: for example, ineffective interventions against the great plague of London included killing dogs, smoking tobacco and burning incense to try and purify the air. All these seemed quite reasonable at the time, but without a detailed understanding of how the disease was passed from rats, to fleas, to humans, they were completely ineffective. Banning drugs assumes that drug problems, or 'addiction', is a disease, caused by the presence of drugs and something must be done to stop them. Writing about obesity, this:

> … expresses a familiar syllogism. Something must be done about X. Y is something. Therefore Y must be done. This syllogism gave America Prohibition, mandatory-minimum sentences, the sentencing disparity between convictions for crack and powder cocaine, and that great guarantee of everyone's security, shoe removal at airports (Lexington, 2012).

Similarly, the disease metaphor has led repeatedly to: premature action on drug problems before there was sufficient evidence to act; irrational persistence with activities that have failed to improve drugs problems; and a focus on cutting-edge things that might work, particularly if they have a biological flavour (e.g. cranial electrical stimulation or vaccines against cocaine), rather than duller things that do work such as psychological therapy.

Policy and practice while drugs are illegal
Staying grounded in the current policy framework, good practice against drug problems is also hindered by thinking focused on the harmfulness of specific substances. As we have noted, in Scotland as in many places most interventions are ostensibly to prevent or treat 'problem drug use', which is supposedly about heroin, cocaine or methamphetamine use. Yet in 2010/11, Scottish police forces seized heroin 3,484 times and cannabis 16,871 times (Henderson, 2012), illustrating that on the ground policies against problem drug use continue to impact mostly on non-problem drug use. This contrasts with the provision of services, which is predominantly about heroin and cocaine.

Prevention
Much health education and health promotion work aims to reduce the prevalence of drug use, on the flawless logic that a person who has never taken, say, heroin cannot become a heroin addict. Unfortunately, most of this work has been based on unachievable objectives that are incoherent and fail to appreciate how young people's attitudes to intoxication develop (Coggans *et al.*, 1991; Hanson, 2007). The common objective of such work is to reduce the number of young people who go on to take drugs. In the 1980s and 90s interventions sometimes addressed drugs without also looking at alcohol and tobacco, although the vast majority of Scots drink.

The objective of reducing drug use is problematic, because, as people grow up between ages eight and twenty-one, the norm is that substance use increases. One may be able to reduce a generation's drug use compared to an older generation, but young people receiving an intervention will almost always increase their substance use anyway. Indeed, discussing and drawing attention to drugs may actually enhance drug trying (Coggans *et al.*, 1991). One reason for this is that younger children have highly negative attitudes to substance use, which are based on common media stereotypes and any experience of adult use (Jessor and Jessor, 1977). Providing drugs education at this stage is almost bound to make attitudes less negative. This could accelerate the natural process whereby children witness their peers trying substances, see that they seem to be fun rather than horrific and consider trying themselves.

Better objectives for prevention would be to slow the rate of drug trying and promote sensible or responsible drug use. Unfortunately, while all alcohol containers in the UK now say 'Drink responsibly' such messages are not allowed for drugs. No drug use is responsible, because, at minimum, it is illegal. This stymies official interventions and means that non-statutory agencies such as Lifeline (www.lifeline. org) can only target people who are already using drugs. Lifeline is among the organisations that are good at providing more nuanced information that may help prevent people developing more problematic patterns of drug use. But, it is questionable whether such information alone is enough.

One aim of general interventions is to prevent supposedly recreational users from converting into addicts or problem drug users. However, general drugs (not alcohol) interventions make little or no distinction between preventing drug problems and preventing drugs. Interventions that do not reduce the prevalence of drugs use are deemed failures. Or rather, because very few interventions demonstrably reduce prevalence, interventions persist, with insistence that they actually do work or will work soon once more of the same is applied with sufficient intensity.

Alcohol, tobacco and drugs

One way forwards to is to address drinking and smoking, hoping that the health and safety messages for these can be applied also to drugs. Progress has been made in doing this, although the relevant industries continue to fight to have alcohol and tobacco isolated from drugs as special cases integral to the economy. The clear message now is not to smoke, and that neither smoking nor drinking are only matters of individual choice, or addiction. School-based drugs education now includes alcohol, tobacco and medicines and is not so often delivered by police officers. It also appropriately tries to integrate substance use into personal, social and health education (Stead *et al.*, 2005). However, a persistent message appears to be that a major reason for avoiding drugs is the risk of addiction. For cannabis, MDMA and so on, this will seem counterfactual to the many young people who have been exposed to use of these drugs. Additionally, the problem remains that adult life in Scotland, witnessed by children, includes drinking – often visible extreme drinking – despite warnings on every alcohol container to drink responsibly. Ideally, there would be a less mixed message.

Cannabis

Purportedly, in many social circles cannabis is barely considered a drug, despite its illegality. It is certainly the only illegal drug widely used by parents and by professional middle-class people, including those involved in law enforcement and anti-drugs work. The current social status of cannabis is rather 'don't ask, don't tell'. Because it is rarely discussed honestly, there is a risk of falling into one of two errors. People tend to assume either that it is safe and non-addictive, and hence can be used liberally unlike alcohol or opiates, ignoring issues of cannabis overuse and dependence, or that it is a 'drug' and should not be used at all. Whatever policy of cannabis-use management there should be, it is currently hindered by its legal status as a Class B drug.

Intoxication versus addiction

There is remarkably little research on why so many people like getting intoxicated, but nonetheless this is a truth overlooked by much policy and practice. Conventional official thinking on this is that people should not want to get intoxicated, and that temperance, even abstinence, is the natural state of humankind (but intoxication is as old as history). Therefore, there is something wrong with people who do want to get intoxicated (but if there is, then it is a common defect). Moreover, much policy continues to assume that addiction inevitably follows habitual intoxication. It is true that all addicts have histories of habitual intoxication, but so do a large minority of people who have never become problem drug users (Orford, 2001; Shewan and Dalgarno, 2005; Ditton and Hammersley, 1996).

These assumptions contain an implicit conventional moral judgement about the wrongness of intoxication, which is commonly held even by people who have been intoxicated themselves, even if it was only while they were at university and they did not enjoy it much. Hypocrisy is not the main problem. Rather, the moral judgement leads to the common policy response to drugs, extreme drinking and so on, which is to try and stop it and, supporting this effort, to seek and document the harms caused by it. This leads to a failure to distinguish the normal morally lamentable behaviours of using intoxicants sometimes, from the unusual and harmful behaviours known as problem drug use (Hammersley, 2011; 2012). There is a need for policies that are more accepting of intoxication and more evidence-based in their appraisal of harms (Nutt *et al.*, 2010).

Systemic factors

As described in the Introduction, Scotland is quite keen on intoxication and inconsistent in the ways that people using drugs are judged. To some extent, addiction is only a social construct used to label negatively certain behaviours by certain types of people (Davies, 1992), because very similar behaviours involving other people and other drugs are more accepted and considered less harmful – notably heavy alcohol use. Someone who consumes as few as two 'tenner bags' of heroin a day will often get a methadone prescription as treatment for their drug problem. Someone who has only two units of alcohol a day is a 'responsible' drinker. Nowadays, many health care professionals would argue that society has not so much singled out drugs for stigmatisation as been excessively complacent about alcohol problems.

Were the social, health and economic problems caused by a drug only as bad as those caused by alcohol, then they would be bad indeed. In the UK, there appear to be many alcohol drinkers who show signs of alcohol dependence, and many more who would probably be judged as dependent if they used another drug to the same extent, but who would object to being labelled addicts or alcoholics. In England in 2011, for example, people who were married or in a relationship, and with gross household weekly incomes of more than £1,000 per week were more likely to drink often, and above safe limits, than people with lower incomes or who were single (NHS Information

Centre, 2011). If this applies also to drug use – and there is some evidence that it does, despite middle-class married people denying such illegal activities in surveys (Ditton and Hammersley, 1996; Shewan and Dalgarno, 2005) – then the bulk of controlled but excessive substance use may occur unnoticed among respectable people, in private.

The most common conceptualisation of this is that there are many hidden and largely unwitting or deluded addicts, who show signs of dependence and who actually require help to moderate or quit their problematic drinking or drug use. Alternatively, perhaps 'signs' of dependence are not coterminous with 'consequences' of dependence, and there exist unknown but probably substantial numbers of people whose substance use fit some criteria for dependence, but who reject the label of addiction and who attempt to control and manage their use to minimise harm (Webb *et al.*, 2007; Shewan and Dalgarno, 2005; Coggans *et al.*, 2004). It seems likely that employment, social support and social capital make it easier to sustain a pattern of heavy substance use without suffering the worst effects.

Under this conceptualisation, the health damage wrought by alcohol and drugs is risked by all users and is more of a public health problem, which still deserves attention. Rather than attacking supposedly 'problem' drugs, there is a need to conceptualise the nature of 'problem drug use' in substance independent ways. The imminent revisions of the *Diagnostic and Statistical Manual of Mental Disorders* and the *WHO International Classification of Diseases* may be moving in this direction.

There is also a need to think more systemically about the ways that drug problems are created by society, both in terms of how they are commonly defined, and how policy and practice help to sustain them in their current forms. Scotland's Futures Forum (2008) developed an innovative systemic way of thinking about drug problems, which input into current government policy. Among the key messages is that changing one thing can unintentionally affect others. For example, liberalising alcohol licensing laws helped create the modern nighttime economy in city centres, where intoxication is celebrated. This in turn has probably maintained a high prevalence of drug use. The hope probably was that liberal alcohol laws would, if anything, promote drinking over drugs.

Social exclusion

Social capital cushions people from the worst effects of excessive drug use, while poverty and social exclusion intensify drug problems in many ways.

First, because drug and, more often, alcohol problems are widespread, it is not unusual for children to grow up with parents or other family members who have substance-use problems. This sets the conditions for the child to develop a problem themselves, because substance-use problems can worsen social exclusion and poverty, contribute to child neglect and abuse, cause bereavement, domestic violence, separation and other trauma for the child. It can also serve as a negative role model, raising tacit norms regarding the level of intoxication that is socially acceptable, leading to the intergenerational transmission of problems. In more affluent families there is more possibility for children to be at least partly protected from substance-use problems because the family has more social capital: for example, a middle-class child exhibiting problems at school due to parental alcoholism may receive concern and counselling rather than being labelled a troublemaker and excluded.

Second, morbidity and mortality are strongly related to poverty and social exclusion, meaning that young people are more likely to have to deal with the premature illness and death of loved ones. We have theorised that trauma can intensify drug use and convert into problem use (Hammersley, 2011).

Third, people tend to be protected against drug problems by having other competing life interests, most importantly education, employment, acquiring a partner and raising a family. This applies across society, but in more affluent areas people increasingly do not attain full adult independence until their mid- to late twenties, whereas in more deprived areas many people have reached full adult status before they are twenty, with a partner, children and their own home. This affects how substance use is moderated by other interests, particularly at the ages of peak use (late teens to mid-twenties). More affluent young people peak their substance use when they are still aspirational – for example, while they are students – so they tend to be motivated to control it in the expectation of life improving. Although more deprived young people reach peak use at similar ages, they are already established, making reconciling substance use and other activities more problematic: for example, the demands of parenting and substance use may cause conflict. There may be no need to restrain drug use for the relatively low-paid job the person has, and little expectation of things getting better.

Fourth, in conditions of poverty and social exclusion, the rewards of drug dealing are more likely to seem attractive and worth the risks (Johnson *et al.*, 1985), and dealing drugs makes it easier for people to develop drug problems.

Thus, drug problems are both a cause and a consequence of social exclusion. However, it would not be easy to prevent drug problems by reducing social exclusion, unless social attitudes to intoxication also changed. Shifting drug preferences, say away from heroin and towards extreme drinking, does not seem like a good outcome. If people's lives can be made sufficiently tolerable that fewer wish to obliterate their memories and worries with intoxication, then that would be a great achievement. Sadly, reducing inequalities in society is not easy or popular. Scotland is about in the middle of developed countries for equality (Grainger and Stewart, 2007) and even in a more equal society bad things still happen to people.

There may be more potential in the careful early identification of children and young people who are at risk of problem drug use, before they actually become drug dependent. Too often, young people receive help only once they have been discovered to have a drug problem, often because they have been caught stealing. This is partly because there are extreme sensitivities about becoming officially known as a drug injector, or admitting that there are substantial problems in the family. Nonetheless, one major route into problem drug use lies in using drugs to escape the aftermath of horrible or traumatic events such as violence and bereavement. When these events are known to have occurred then young people should be helped to recover from the trauma.

There is the difficulty that far more young people fit the profile of possibly developing a drug problem then actually go on to develop one (Hammersley, 2011). As competent services already know, there is often a need to work beyond a person's drug use rather than simply blaming the drug for the problems. In fact, we suggest that drug and alcohol problems are fundamentally problems of inequality and social exclusion, not problems pertaining only to the psychopharmacological properties of drugs.

Should this proposition seem far-fetched, recall that until relatively recently the problems due to the inequality and social exclusion of women were by and large considered to be primarily due to biological differences between men and women (Fausto-Sterling, 1992). Women were deemed delicate, unintelligent, incapable of many activities of which they are extremely capable when inequalities in education and expectations are reduced, biologically driven to focus on child-rearing, etc. etc. Nowadays, female literacy is a major route to lift entire communities from poverty; women's academic performance often surpasses men's; and many women are choosing to delay, or avoid, the traditional life path of marriage and children. Addressing gender inequalities has greatly reduced the problems formerly attributed to 'being a woman'.

Inequalities and drugs

What are the inequalities that cause and are caused by drug problems? More research is needed, but a number of things clearly need to change:

- stigmatisation of specific drugs and drug practices, notably heroin injecting;
- consequent failure to implement a care planning approach with clients who use drugs;
- dismissal of serious drug problems as some form of immorality or lifestyle choice, when drug dependence is a complex mental health problem;
- complacency about other drugs and drug practices (e.g. alcohol and cannabis), especially as complacency about cannabis is increasing;
- focusing excessively on substance use, or abstinence, at the expense of the other personal and social challenges of recovery.

There is a need for more psychological and social research seeking to understand and explain substance use. Most research on drugs both in terms of publications and funding is biomedical and is aimed at understanding how chemicals interact with physiology with a view to modelling the impact of drugs on health and disease (Hammersley and Reid, 2002). Given the scale of biomedical research, there have been scant resultant advances in the policy and practice of reducing drug use, drug problems and drug-related harms. Most of the advances have been due to the application of psychological and sociological understandings to drug problems. This had led to the containment of HIV infection, to effective psychotherapeutic interventions including cognitive behavioural therapy and motivational interviewing, and to the intelligent use of naloxone to prevent overdose.

Research considering human substance use is relatively rare, even considering use in simple terms of how, why, when, where, in what quantity, with what frequency and with whom drugs or alcohol are consumed. Moreover, funding is often politically motivated both in terms of real politics – as practised by politicians – and in terms of more subtle and informal assumptions about what is 'politically' acceptable and unacceptable. Research on human drug use has been particularly hindered by reluctance to ask about tobacco, alcohol, drugs and other health-related behaviours in the same survey for fear of causing offence. Also, there has been a general failure to theorise 'addiction' as a psychological and social problem, rather than a biomedical one. The disease metaphor is not an explanation of why people use drugs.

There is also a problematic bias towards reporting results that document drug-related harms. This bias often extends to a reduction in scientific standards when it comes to publishing findings that accord to current prejudices – the polite phrase is 'seem important' – and will look good in research funders' press releases. Consequently, for the illegal drugs it is extremely difficult to distinguish between true harms that need consideration in policy and practice, and spurious or exaggerated harms that simply encourage bans on drugs that may magnify harm rather than reduce it. These problems are not restricted to minor or obscure harms. Does cannabis trigger schizophrenia, for example, or is does it just affect the reporting of psychotic 'symptoms'? Is cocaine highly addictive, or can most extreme users quit unaided?

Safer drug use

Throughout recorded history people have gone to a lot of trouble to cultivate, manufacture and import the drugs that they like. The drugs chosen, and avoided, are central to many cultures. In the UK, for example, the pub has long been an important part of social life, while in the USA the tensions between alcohol temperance and intoxication helped to shape modern America. Equivalent tensions continue over cannabis, and the USA is both the world's largest consumer of illegal drugs and their most fervent opponent. Tensions intensified in the twentieth century, as a diversity of drugs became available.

A lot of the history of alcohol, tobacco and drugs has been about pretending that some drug use is not really about intoxication at all, for the drug is a food, a charming tradition, an occasional mild social facilitator or entirely harmless, and that other drug use is driven primarily by addiction to that specific substance. Consequently, many societies' only overt rules about intoxication are that it is bad and should not happen. Even rules that ostensibly permit drug use tend to incidentally limit inebriation and exclude intoxication: two drinks a day; cannabis for medical use.

To accommodate inebriation and intoxication in as healthy and safe a manner as possible, it will be necessary to have more mature discussions about what is and is not appropriate. Currently, the main publicly proffered alternative is to glow with well-being and happiness, possibly facilitated by the religion of your preference, mindfulness and vigorous exercise. Unfortunately, in our experience many people glowing in this manner choose to celebrate that exceptional occasion with an inebriant of their choice.

Safer inebriation

The mature discussion would involve consideration that some drugs in some forms may be too dangerous to health and safety to be permitted. But if they are to be banned then other inebriants may be needed in their place. Top candidates for banning include smoked tobacco and injecting opiates, but the list could be much longer.

There also appear to be some general principles regarding how to use drugs more safely. These are not exciting enough to ring of 'scientific discovery', but they are nonetheless important:

- Drug preparations should be of known purity.
- Stronger drug preparations are more dangerous than weaker ones and ideally should be priced and controlled accordingly.
- Methods of consumption that allow the user fine control over dose are safer.
- No drug can be taken daily, particularly to intoxication, with indefinite impunity, and wishing to do this is a warning sign of psychological and social problems.
- People who turn to drugs to cope with life's miseries would benefit from help with those miseries, when possible.
- People tend to control their drug use when they have good reasons to do so and fail to control it when they do not care (Hammersley, 2012).
- Making a drug more legally available means use is more widespread, but safer.
- Legal industries can be taxed and regulated in response to problems with their products; illegal ones cannot.

Social norms for intoxication

While teaching and presenting on drugs, we have discussed norms with a lot of people. Here are some points about intoxication to which few people object and that can be applied to all intoxicants:

- The advertising and other avid promotion of intoxicants, including alcohol and tobacco (e.g. in lurid media stories) is wrong. One might include over-the-counter medicines in a ban, as their adverts send a message that drugs are alright if you do not feel well and the psychological distance from 'pain' to 'sadness' is not very far. However, the incidental portrayal of alcohol drinking in the media as an everyday occurrence without consequences is also a problem.
- People should not be placed in social situations in which they feel obliged to consume intoxicants, even when others are doing so.
- Under a certain age children should not use intoxicants, except perhaps in very moderate doses under direct parental

supervision. What age is a tricky question, but somewhere between sixteen and twenty-one is a rough consensus. It is inevitable that some children will use them below the legal age, but this is to be discouraged and considered in sensible lawmaking. A big disadvantage of making a drug illegal is that this age differentiation is not possible.

- Using an intoxicant daily is likely to cause problems and should be avoided. Being intoxicated most of the day is even more likely to cause problems. Habitual users see use as routine and tend to underestimate the risks of it.

- If daily use occurs then it is important to have strict limits how much, when and where it is used; perhaps a key factor in medical use.

- Intoxicants should not be used while working or in other situations demanding care and attention, such as driving.

- Intoxicants should not be used frequently to the extent that they lead to loss of consciousness, feeling unwell or being unable to function the following day.

- Intoxicants should not be used in ways that are a regular burden to other people, which includes failing to fulfil ones duties, needing looked after and becoming a bore or a nuisance.

- It is widely but far from universally acceptable to get extremely intoxicated occasionally, which can be as often as once or twice a week for some people, although this is probably too often. However, there are always anxieties about this escalating to more problematic use, about accidents and harms while intoxicated and about long-term health damage.

- When people regularly get much more intoxicated than those around them, this should be cause for concern.

- People should only consume intoxicants as much as they can reasonably afford.

Violations of all but the first two norms tend to suggest that the person has problems with intoxicant use. Adverse medical effects appear on this list, but they do not dominate it, for they do not dominate drug choices.

Conclusions

The future will contain problem drug use, but not necessarily in current forms, because the causes of problem drug use, including trauma and social exclusion, will not disappear. Eventually more drugs will be regulated, rather than banned, and it would be helpful if this were done in an evidence-based manner. However, it is likely that the drugs eventually regulated will be those for which there is most demand, rather than from a rational cost-benefit analysis. Attacking the specific drugs involved in drug problems is not a highly productive activity, and it displaces thinking away from the root causes of drug problems. The disease metaphor of addiction and the common consequent circular drug-centred thinking has impeded rational policies. Policy and practice have moved towards focus on the person who has a drug problem, rather than just concentrating on the drug, but there needs to be much more consideration of the broader context of drug use in society and what this means, and should mean, for the prevention and management of drug problems. Inebriation and intoxication are integral to society in Scotland and pretending that they are not, or requiring them not to be, are not sensible ways forwards.

REFERENCES

Agar, M. (1973) *Ripping and Running: A Formal Ethnography of Urban Heroin Addicts*, New York: Seminar Press

Aldridge, J., Measham, F. and Williams, L. (2011) *Illegal leisure revisited. Changing patterns of alcohol and drug use in adolescents and young adults.* London: Routledge

Allen, J. P., Mattson, M. E., Miller, W. R., Tonigan, J. S., Connors, G. J., Rychtarik, R. G. *et al.* (1999) 'Summary of Project MATCH', *Addiction,* Vol. 94, No. 1, pp. 31–4

Amos, A., Wiltshire, S., Bostock, Y., Haw, S. and McNeill, A. (2004) ' "You can't go without a fag ... you need it for your hash" – a qualitative exploration of smoking, cannabis and young people', *Addiction,* Vol. 99, No. 1, pp. 77–81

Anderson, T. and Levy, J. A (2003) 'Marginality among older injectors in today's illicit drug culture: assessing the impact of ageing', *Addiction,* Vol. 98, No. 6, pp. 761–70

Arrindell, W. (2001) 'Changes in waiting-list patients over time: Data on some commonly-used measures. beware!', *Behaviour Research and Therapy,* Vol. 39, No. 10, pp. 1227–47

Avert (2012) *UK HIV diagnoses by transmission route.* Available at URL: www.avert.org/uk-transmission-route.htm (accessed 13 January 2012)

Barr, A. (1995) *Drink: An Informal Social History*, London: Bantam Press

BBC News (2007) 'Heroin treatment at record levels'. Available at URL: http://news.bbc.co.uk/1/hi/scotland/6911012.stm (accessed 3 March 2010)

Bean, P. (2004) *Drugs and Crime,* Cullompton: Willan, 2nd edn

Beck, A. T., Wright, F. D., Newman, C. F. and Liese, B. S. (1993) *Cognitive Therapy of Substance Abuse*, New York: Guilford Press

Bell, D. N. F. and Blanchflower, D. G. (2010) *Young People and Recession. A Lost Generation?* Economic Policy, Fifty-Second Annual Meeting, Paris. Available at URL: www.cepr.org/meets/wkcn/9/979/papers/Bell_%20Blanchflower.pdf (accessed 8 May 2012)

Best, D. (2009) *Mapping Routes to Recovery and the Role of Recovery Groups and Communities.* Presentation to STRADA. Available at URL: www.fead.org.uk/docs/STRADAMasterclass_DavidBest.pdf (accessed 29 February 2012)

Borio, G. (2003) *The Tobacco Timeline.* Available at URL: www.tobacco.org/History/Tobacco_History.html (accessed 10 October 2007)

Boussel, P., Bonnemain, H. and Bove, R. (1983) *History of Pharmacy and the Pharmaceutical Industry*, Paris: Asklepios

Buning, E. (1994) 'Methadone in Europe', *International Journal of Drug Policy*, Vol. 5, p. 4

Castells, M. (1998) *End of Millennium*, Oxford: Blackwell

CNN (2000) *A Brief History of Tobacco*. Available at URL: www.cnn.com/ US/9705/tobacco/history/index.html (accessed 20 June 2012)

Coggans, N., Dalgarno, P., Johnson, L. and Shewan, D. (2004) 'Long-term heavy cannabis use: Implications for health education', *Drugs: Education, Prevention and Policy*, Vol. 11, pp. 299–313

Coggans, N., Shewan, D., Henderson, M. and Davies, J. B. (1991) *National Evaluation of Drug Education in Scotland.* ISDD Research Monograph Four, London: Institute for the Study of Drug Dependence

Dalai Lama and Cutler, H. C. (2009) *The Art of Happiness: A Handbook for Living,* London: Hodder, 10th anniversary edn

Davies, J. B. (1992) *The Myth of Addiction.* Reading: Harwood

De Paula, R. S. (2004) 'What can we learn from psychoanalysis and prospective studies about chemically dependent patients?', *International Journal of Psychoanalysis,* Vol. 85, No. 2, pp. 467–87

Dee J (2007) 'Exporting ignorance: The American way', *Soft Secrets,* (UK edn; Amsterdam), Vol. 2 (March), p. 39

Department of Health (2008) *Refocusing the Care Programme Approach. Policy and Positive Practice Guidance*, London: Department of Health

Department of Health, Scottish Office Home and Health Department, Welsh Office (1991) *Drug Misuse and Dependence: Guidelines on Clinical Management,* London: HMSO

Derricott, J., Preston, A. and Hunt, N. (1999) *The Safer Injecting Briefing,* Liverpool: HIT. Available from URL: www.exchangesupplies.org/drug_information/briefings/the_safer_injecting_briefing/preface.html (accessed 8 May 2012)

Ditton, J. and Hammersley, R. (1996) *A Very Greedy Drug: Cocaine in Context.* Reading: Harwood

Ditton, J. and Taylor, A. (1987) *Scotland Drugs Resource Book, 1980–84,* Glasgow: Criminology Research Unit, University of Glasgow

DMIS (2008) *Drug Misuse Statistics Scotland, 2008,* C3.1 SPS Addictions Prevalence Testing 2007/08. Available at URL: www.drugmisuse.isdscotland.org/ publications/08dmss/08dmss-115.htm (accessed 8 May 2012)

Douglas, M. and Wildavsky, A. (1983) *Risk and Culture: An Essay on the Selection of Technological and Environmental Dangers,* San Francisco: University of California Press

Dreyfuss, R. (1999) 'George W. Bush: Calling for Philip Morris', *The Nation,* New York, 21 October

Drug Policy Commission Recovery Consensus Group (2008) *A Vision of Recovery,* London: UK Drugs Policy Commission

EKOS (2009) *The Experience of Rural Poverty in Scotland: Qualitative Research with Organisations Working with People Experiencing Poverty in Rural Areas,* Edinburgh: Scottish Government

Ericson, R. (2006) *Crime in an Insecure World,* London: Polity

Everitt, B. J., Dickinson, A. and Robbins, T. W. (2001) 'The neuropsychological basis of addictive behaviour', *Brain Research Reviews,* Vol. 36, Nos 2–3 special issue, pp. 129–38

Executive Office of the President of the USA (2004) *The Economic Costs of Drug*

Abuse in the United States, 1992–2002. Washington: Executive Office of the President. Available at URL: https://www.ncjrs.gov/ondcppubs/publications/pdf/economic_costs.pdf (accessed 21 June 2012)

Fausto-Sterling, A. (1992) *Myths of Gender: Biological Theories About Men and Women,* New York: Basic Books

Feldman, E. A. and Bayer, R. (eds) (2004) *Unfiltered: Conflicts Over Tobacco Policy and Public Health,* Cambridge MA: Harvard University Press

Forsyth, A. J. M., Cloonan, M. and Barr, J. (2005) *Factors Associated with Alcohol-Related Problems with Licensed Premises,* report to Greater Glasgow NHS Board. Available at URL: http://library.nhsgg.org.uk/mediaAssets/library/nhsgg_pilp_main_report_2005–02.pdf (accessed 11 September 2007)

Forsyth, A. J. M., Khan, F. and McKinlay, B. (2011) 'Alcohol and diazepam use among male Young Offenders: "The Devil's Mixture" ', *Drugs Education Prevention and Policy,* Vol. 18, pp. 468–76

Frischer, M., Goldberg, D., Taylor, A., and Bloor, M. (1997) 'Estimating the incidence and prevalence of injecting drug use in Glasgow', *Addiction Research,* Vol. 5, No. 4, pp. 307–15

Funada, M. (2010) 'Pharmacological properties and dependence liabilities of synthetic cannabinoids', *Japanese Journal of Alcohol Studies & Drug Dependence,* Vol. 45, No. 3, pp. 167–74

General Register of Scotland (2012) *Drug-Related Deaths in Scotland, 2010.* Available at URL: www.gro-scotland.gov.uk/files2/stats/drug-related-deaths/2010 (accessed 8 May 2012)

Grainger, S., and Stewart, S. (2007) *Income Distribution in Scotland.* Scottish Economic Statistics, 2007. Edinburgh: Scottish Government. Available at URL: www.scotland.gov.uk/Publications/2007/07/18083820/4 (accessed 12 July 2012)

Gruer, L., Cameron, J. and Elliott, L. (1993) 'Building a city wide service for exchanging needles and syringes', *British Medical Journal,* Vol. 306, No. 6889, pp. 1394–7

Hammersley, R. (2009) *Drugs and Crime: Theory and Practice.* Cambridge: Polity

Hammersley, R. (2010) 'Dangers of banning spice and synthetic cannabinoids' (letter), *Addiction,* Vol. 105, No. 2, pp. 373–5

Hammersley, R. (2011) 'Pathways through drugs and crime: Risk, resilience and diversity', *Journal of Criminal Justice;* doi:10.1016/j.jcrimjus.2011.02.006

Hammersley, R. (2012) *Constraint Theory: Towards a Psychological, Motivational, Teleological Theory of the Setting of Dependence.* Working Paper. Hull: University of Hull. Available at URL: http://hull.academia.edu/RichardHammersley/Papers/1155470/constraint_theory_of_dependence_rhh (accessed 21 June 2012)

Hammersley, R. and Dalgarno, P. (2012) '*I Love the Feeling Drugs Give, I Just Can't Take Them.*' *Pathways To Recovery Amongst People Who Have Injected Drugs Within the Past Five Years,* Final Report to the Big Lottery Research Fund, Edinburgh: Scottish Drugs Forum

Hammersley, R. and Pearl, S. (1996) 'Drug use and other problems of residents in projects for the young, single homeless', *Health and Social Care in the Com-*

munity, Vol. 4, pp. 193–9

Hammersley, R. and Reid, M. (2002) 'Why the pervasive addiction myth is still believed', *Addiction Research and Theory*, Vol. 10, pp. 7–30

Hammersley, R., Cassidy, M. T. and Oliver, J. (1995) 'Drugs associated with drug-related deaths in Edinburgh and Glasgow November 1990 to October 1992', *Addiction,* Vol. 90, pp. 959–65

Hammersley, R., Forsyth, A. J. M, Morrison, V. L. and Davies, J. B. (1989) 'The relationship between crime and opioid use', *British Journal of Addiction,* Vol. 84, pp. 1029–43

Hammersley, R., Kahn, F. and Ditton, J. (2002) *Ecstasy and the Rise of the Chemical Generation*, Reading, Harwood

Hanson, D. J. (2007) *Drug Abuse Resistance Education: The Effectiveness of DARE.* Available at URL: http://alcoholfacts.org/DARE.html (accessed 17 July 2012)

Haw, S. (1985) *Drug Problems in Greater Glasgow*, Glasgow: Scottish Council on Drugs and Alcohol

Hay, G., Gannon, M., Casey, J. and McKeganey, N. (2009) *Estimating the National and Local Prevalence of Problem Drug Misuse in Scotland*, Glasgow: University of Glasgow. Available at URL: www.drugmisuse.isdscotland.org/publications/abstracts/prevalence2009.htm (accessed 21 June 2012)

Health Protection Agency, Health Protection Scotland, National Public Health Service for Wales, CDSC (2008) *Shooting Up: Infections Among Injecting Drug Users in the United Kingdom 2007*, London: Health Protection Agency

HEAT (2010) *HEAT Target.* Available at URL: www.scotland.gov.uk/Topics/Justice/law/Drugs-Strategy/recovery/HEAT (accessed 29 February 2012)

Henderson, N. (2012) *Drug Seizures by Scottish Police Forces, 2010–11.* Statistical Bulletin, Crime and Justice Series. Edinburgh, Scottish Government. Available at URL: www.scotland.gov.uk/Resource/0039/00391948.pdf (accessed 20 June 2012)

Hepburn, M. (1998) 'Drug use in pregnancy: A multidisciplinary responsibility', *Hospital Medicine*, Vol. 59, No. 6, p. 436

Hill, M., Walker, M., Moodie, K., Wallace, B., Bannister, J., Khan, F. *et al.* (2005) *Fast Track Children's Hearing Pilot: Final Report of the Evaluation of the Pilot (abridged version)*, Edinburgh: Scottish Executive

Hiro, D. (2001) 'Wasteful battle for the holy soil of Arabia', *Guardian*. Available at URL: www.guardian.co.uk/waronterror/story/0,,573786,00.html (accessed 20 June 2012)

Hunt, L. G. and Chambers, C. D. (1976) *The Heroin Epidemics: A Study of Heroin Use in the U.S., Part 2, 1965–75*, Holliswood, NY: Spectrum

Information Services Edinburgh (2007) *Drug Misuse Statistics Scotland 2007,* Edinburgh: Information Services. Available at URL: www.drugmisuse.isdscotland.org/publications/07dmss/07dmss.pdf (accessed 17 July 2012)

Inside Time (2009) *Drugs in Prison.* Available at URL: www.insidetime.org/articleview.asp?a=563&c=drugs_in_prison (accessed 16 February 2012)

ISD Scotland (1998) *Drug Misuse Statistics Scotland.* Available at URL: www.drugmisuse.isdscotland.org/publications/98bull/index.htm (accessed 3 March 2010)

ISD Scotland (2002) *Drug Misuse Statistics Scotland.* Available at URL: www. drugmisuse.isdscotland.org/publications/01bull/full/fulldoc.pdf (accessed 10 March 2011)

ISD Scotland (2005) *How Many People Are Prescribed Methadone?* Available at URL: www.drugmisuse.isdscotland.org/publications/local/isd_methadone. pdf (accessed 3 March 2010)

Jessor, R. and Jessor, S. L. (1977) 'The social-psychological framework', in Jessor, R. and Jessor, S. L. (eds) (1977) *Problem Behaviour and Psychosocial Development: A Longitudinal Study of Youth*, New York, NY: Academic Press, pp.17–42

Johnson, B. D., Goldstein, P .J., Preble, E., Schmeidler, J., Liption, D. S., Spunt, B. and Miller, T. (1985) *Taking Care of Business. The Economics of Crime by Heroin Abusers*, Lexington, MA: Lexington Books

Kelso, P. (2002) 'A pint, a dram or a fry-up: how drinking dens made the desert feel like home', *Guardian*. Available at URL: www.guardian.co.uk/inter-national/story/0,,641449,00.html (accessed 20 June 2012)

Klee, H. (1992) 'A new target for behavioural-research – amphetamine misuse', *British Journal of Addiction*, Vol. 87, No. 3, pp. 439–46

Leon, D. and McCambridge, J. (2006) 'Liver cirrhosis mortality rates in Britain, 1950 to 2002', *Lancet,* Vol. 367, No. 9511, p. 645

Lexington (2012) 'Stick or carrot?', *The Economist*, 9 June, p. 44

Ling, P. M. and Glantz, S. A. (2002) 'Using tobacco-industry marketing research to design more effective tobacco-control campaigns', *Journal of the American Medical Association,* Vol. 287, No. 22, pp. 2983–9

Mackay, J. and Eriksen, M. (2002) *The Tobacco Atlas*, Geneva: World Health Organization. Available at URL: www.who.int/tobacco/statistics/tobacco_ atlas/en (accessed 12 July 2012)

MacLeod, P. and Page, L. (2011) *2009/10 Scottish Crime and Justice Survey: Drug Use*, Edinburgh: Scottish Government

Maruna, S. (2008) *Making Good: How Ex-Convicts Reform*, Washington, DC: American Psychological Association

McCoard, S., Skellington Orr, K., Shirley, A. and McCartney, P. (2010) *Process Evaluation of the Drug Treatment and Testing Orders II (DTTO II) Pilots*, Edinburgh: Scottish Government Social Research. Available at URL: www. scotland.gov.uk/Resource/Doc/310418/0097967.pdf (accessed 20 June 2012)

McIvor, G., Barnsdale, L., Eley, S., Malloch, M., Yates, R. and Brown, A. (2006) *An Evaluation of the Glasgow and Fife Drug Courts and Their Aim to Reduce Drug Use and Drug Related Reoffending*, Edinburgh: Scottish Government. Available at URL: www.scotland.gov.uk/Publications/2006/03/28112035/0 (accessed 29 February 2012)

McKeganey, N. (2011) *Controversies in Drugs Policy and Practice*, Cambridge: Palgrave

McKeganey, N. and Barnard, M. (1992a) *AIDS, Drugs and Sexual Risk – Lives in the Balance*, Buckingham, Open University Press

McKeganey, N., and Barnard, M. (1992b) 'Selling sex – female street pros-titution and hiv risk behaviour in Glasgow', *Aids Care-Psychological and Socio-Medical Aspects of Aids/hiv,* Vol. 4, No. 4, pp. 395–407

McKellar, J., Stewart, E. and Humphreys, K. (2003) 'Alcoholics anonymous involvement and positive alcohol-related outcomes: Cause, consequence, or just a correlate? A prospective 2-year study of 2,319 alcohol-dependent men', *Journal of Consulting and Clinical Psychology,* Vol. 71, No. 2, pp. 302–8

Merrall, E. L. C., Kariminia, A., Binswanger, I. A., Hobbs, M. S., Farrell, M., Marsden, J. *et al.* (2010) 'Meta-analysis of drug-related deaths soon after release from prison', *Addiction,* Vol. 105, No. 9, pp. 1545–54

Miller, W. R. and Rollnick, S. (1991) *Motivational Interviewing: Preparing People to Change Addictive Behaviour,* London: Guliford Press

Miller, W. R. and Sanchez-Craig, M. (1996) 'How to have a high success rate in treatment: Advice for evaluators of alcoholism programs', *Addiction,* Vol. 91, No. 6, pp. 779–85

Mitchell, S. (2005) *Gilgamesh. A New English Version,* London: Profile Books

Mullen, K. (1993) *A Healthy Balance: Glaswegian Men Talking about Health, Tobacco and Alcohol,* Aldershot: Avebury

Naim, M. (2005) *Illicit: How Smugglers, Traffickers and Copycats Are Hijacking the Global Economy,* New York: Arrow

Neale, J. (2000) *Drug Users in Society,* Basingstoke: Palgrave

NHS Information Centre (2011) *Statistics on Alcohol, England, 2011.* Available at URL: www.ic.nhs.uk (accessed 29 February 2012)

NHS ISD (2011) *Estimating the National and Local Prevalence of Problem Drug Use in Scotland.* Edinburgh: Information Services Division. Available at URL: www.isdscotland.org/Health-Topics/Drugs-and-Alcohol-Misuse/Publications/2011-11-29/2011-11-29-DrugPrevalence-Summary.pdf?38367861510 (accessed 20 June 2012)

Nutt D. J., King L. A. and Phillips L. D. (2010) 'Drug harms in the UK: a multicriteria decision analysis', *Lancet,* Vol. 376, pp. 1558–65

Orford, J. (2001) *Excessive Appetites: A Psychological View of the Addictions,* London: Wiley, 2nd edn

Penfold, C., Turnbull, P. J. and Webster, R. (2005) *Tackling Prison Drug Markets: An Exploratory Qualitative Study,* Home Office Online Report 39/05. London: Home Office

Plant, M. (1975) *Drug-Takers in an English Town,* London: Tavistock

Roberts, P. (2001) *Review of Fairground Safety,* Report to the Health and Safety Executive. Available at URL: www.hse.gov.uk/entertainment/pdf/revrep.pdf (accessed 8 May 2012)

Robertson, R. (1987) *Heroin, AIDS and Society,* London: Hodder Arnold

RSA (2007) *Drugs–facing Facts: The Report of the RSA Commission on Illegal Drugs, Communities and Public Policy,* London: Royal Society for the encouragement of Arts, Manufactures and Commerce

Runciman, R. [ed] (1999) *Drugs and the Law: Report of the Independent Inquiry into the Misuse of Drugs Act 1971.* London: Police Foundation. Available at URL: www.druglibrary.org/schaffer/Library/studies/runciman/default.htm (accessed 31 May 2007)

Schaffer Library of Drug Policy (2009) *The Indian Hemp Drugs Commission Report.* Available at URL: www.druglibrary.org/Schaffer/library/studies/inhemp/ihmenu.htm (accessed 6 October 2009)

Scotland's Futures Forum (2008) *Approaches to Alcohol and Drugs in Scotland. A Question of Architecture*, Edinburgh: Scotland's Futures Forum

Scottish Government (2008) *The Road to Recovery: A New Approach to Tackling Scotland's Drug Problem*, Edinburgh: Scottish Government

Scottish Government (2012) *Income and Poverty Statistics Web Area*. Available at URL: www.scotland.gov.uk/Topics/Statistics/Browse/Social-Welfare/ IncomePoverty (accessed 28 June 2012)

SDRC (2011) *Key Messages*, Glasgow: Scottish Drugs Recovery Consortium. Available at URL: www.sdrconsortium.org/index.php?id=145 (accessed 1 March 2012)

Seivewright, N. (2000) *Community Treatment of Drug Misuse: More Than Methadone*, Cambridge: Cambridge University Press

SGSR (2012) *2010/11 Scottish Crime and Justice Survey: Drug Use*, Edinburgh: Scottish Government Social Research. Available at URL: www.scotland.gov. uk/Resource/0039/00390472.pdf (accessed 20 June 2012)

Shewan, D. and Dalgarno, P. (2005) 'Evidence for controlled heroin use? Low levels of negative health and social outcomes among non-treatment heroin users in Glasgow (Scotland)', *British Journal of Health Psychology*, Vol. 10, No. 1, pp. 33–48

Simpson, D. D. and Friend, J. (1988) 'Legal status and long-term outcomes from addicts in the DARP follow-up project', in Leukefield, C. G. and Tims, F. M. (eds) (1988) *Compulsory Treatment of Drug Abuse*, National Institute of Drug Abuse Research Monographs, No. 86, Rockville, MD: US Department of Health and Human Services, pp. 81–98

Smith, R. (2006) *The Utility of Force: The Art of War in the Modern World*, London: Penguin

Sobell, M. B. and Sobell, L. C. (2006) 'Obstacles to the adoption of low risk drinking goals in the treatment of alcohol problems in the United States: A commentary', *Addiction Research and Theory*, Vol. 14, No. 1, pp. 19–24

Stallard, A., Hammersley, R., Elliott, L. and Horne, A. (1998) *A Peer Assisted Risk Reduction Programme For Residents at a Crisis Intervention Centre. Final Report to the Chief Scientist Office*, Scotland, Edinburgh: Chief Scientist Office

Standage, T. (2007) *A History of the World in Six Glasses*, London: Atlantic

Stead, M., MacKintosh, A. M., McDermott, L., Eadie, D., Macnell, M., Stradling, R. and Minty, S. (2005) *Evaluation of the effectiveness of drug education in Scottish schools*, Edinburgh: Scottish Executive. Available at URL: www. scotland.gov.uk/Resource/Doc/96353/0023319.pdf (accessed 19 June 2012)

Stevens, A. (2010) 'Evidence and policy: Crime and public health in UK drug policy', in Yates, R and Malloch, M. S. [eds] (2010) *Tackling Addiction: Pathways to Recovery*. London; Jessica Kingsley, pp 156–74

Strang, J. and Sheridan, J. (1997) 'Heroin prescribing in the "British system" of the mid-1990s: Data from the 1995 national survey of community pharmacies in England and Wales', *Drug and Alcohol Review*, Vol. 16, No. 1, pp. 7–16

STV (2010) 'Politicians hit out over methadone use in prisons'. Available at URL: http://news.stv.tv/scotland/181004-politicians-hit-out-over-methadone-use-in-prisons (accessed 8 May 2012)

Szasz, T. (1974) *Ceremonial Chemistry: The Ritual Persecution of Drugs, Addicts, and Pushers*, Syracuse, NY: Syracuse University Press

Taylor, A. (1994) *Women Drug Users: An Ethnography of a Female Injecting Community*, Oxford: Oxford University Press

Taylor, A., Champion, J. and Fleming, A. (2006) *The Role of Methadone Maintenance in Scottish Prisons: Prisoners' Perspectives.* Edinburgh: Scottish Prison Service. Available at URL: www.drugslibrary.stir.ac.uk/documents/spsmeth.pdf (accessed 8 May 2012)

Templeton, L., Zohhadi, S., Galvani, S. and Velleman, R. (2006) *'Looking Beyond risk' Parental Substance Misuse: Scoping Study*, Edinburgh: Scottish Executive

Thoumi, F. E. (2005) 'The numbers game: Let's all guess the size of the illegal drug industry!', *Journal of Drug Issues*, Vol. 35, No. 1, pp. 185–200

United Nations Office on Drugs and Crime (2006) *World Drug Report*, New York: United Nations, Vols 1 and 2

Vaillant, G. E. (1995) *The Natural History of Alcoholism Revisited*, Cambridge, MA: Harvard University Press

Webb, H., Rolfe, A., Orford, J., Painter, C. and Dalton, S. (2007) 'Self-directed change or specialist help? Understanding the pathways to changing drinking in heavy drinkers', *Addiction Research and Theory*, Vol. 15. No. 1, pp. 85–95

Wejnert, C., Pham, H., Oster, A. M., DiNenno, E. A., Smith, A., Krishna, N. and Lansky, A. (2012) *HIV Infection and HIV-Associated Behaviors Among Injecting Drug Users – 20 Cities, United States, 2009*, Atlanta, GA: Centers for Disease Control and Prevention. Available at URL: www.cdc.gov/mmwr/preview/mmwrhtml/mm6108a1.htm#tab1 (accessed 20 March 2012)

WHO (1993) *WHO Guidelines on HIV and AIDS in Prisons*, Geneva: World Health Organization

Wight, D. (1993) *Workers Not Wasters*, Edinburgh: Edinburgh University Press

Wikipedia (2012) 'Margaret Thatcher'. Available at URL: http://en.wikipedia.org/wiki/Margaret_Thatcher (accessed 21 June 2012)

Williams, M., Teasdale, J., Segal, Z., Kabat-Zinn, J. (2007) *The Mindful Way Through Depression: Freeing Yourself From Chronic Unhappiness*, London: Guilford Press

Yates, R and Malloch, M. S. (2010) *Tackling Addiction: Pathways to Recovery*, London: Jessica Kingsley

INDEX